Collecting Victorian Jewellery

By the same author

—

COLLECTING VICTORIANA

Miss Jenny Lind. Steel engraving, *c.* 1850. *Collection of Miss May Giles.*

Collecting
Victorian Jewellery

——

MARY PETER

Emerson Books Inc. New York

Published 1971 by Emerson Books, Inc.
Standard Book Number: 87523–174–8
Library of Congress Catalog Card Number: 78–137400

Acknowledgements

THIS BOOK owes a great deal to the very generous help I have received, both from private collectors and museums.

The Birmingham City Art Gallery, the Plymouth City Art Gallery, the Royal Institution of Cornwall (Truro) and the Victoria and Albert Museum have kindly allowed me to reproduce pieces from their collections. I am especially grateful for the scholarly help of Miss Glennys Wild at Birmingham.

I am indebted to Mr Martin J. Desmoni and Mr Raphael Esmerian of New York for lending me transparencies and photographs from their collections of jewellery by Castellani and Carlo Giuliano, also for very kind advice and information. Mr Desmoni and Mr Esmerian have taken great trouble to help me, for which I am truly grateful.

I am indebted also to the many collectors in this country who have lent me their jewellery to be photographed or drawn. Mr William Andrew, Miss Child, Miss May Giles, Mrs Charles Girling, Miss Josephine Harris, Mr Louis Jolly, Mrs Kingerley, Mrs Bryan Pearce, Mr and Mrs Penna, Mrs E. M. Phillips, Dr Donald Towle M.D., Mrs Philip Varcoe and Mrs Philip Williams, have not only put their Victorian pieces completely at my disposal, but helped most kindly in other ways as well.

Mr Larsen, Mr Wyman, Mr Woolf and Mr Hill have shewn unfailing patience over photographing some difficult pieces and Birmingham City Art Gallery took special care over their photographs. To Mrs S. M. Isaacs, who has coped with typing from very indifferent manuscript, and to my sister Jenefer, who did the drawings, I owe a special debt of gratitude.

Lastly, I am especially indebted to Lady Mander and Miss Griffiths for the restoring hospitality of Wightwick. To the atmosphere of Wightwick, best of Victorian houses, this book owes a great deal.

7

Contents

Plates

11

12   Demi-Parure. Brooch and Earrings in ivory, *c.* 1870-80.

13   Late Victorian Brooches and a Pendant. *Top*; Buckle Brooch Scottish pebble in silver, *c.* 1890; *centre*: Brooch, Cupid with Lyre, in malachite and silver, *c.* 1898; Pendant, gold with beryls, in *art nouveau* style, *c.* 1890; Brooch, soapstone with turquoise and gold, *c.* 1898; *below*: Bar Brooch, *c.* 1880, malachite and gold.

14   Jet faceted Necklace and three Brooches: *top*: Celtic cross shape; *centre*: with white porcelain; *below*: faceted jet mount with crystal. All *c.* 1870–80.

15   Coral Pins and a Brooch. *Left*: Stock or Tie Pin, *centre*: Brooch, coral, enamel and gold, *c.* 1850-60; *right*: Pin, coral and gold, *c.* 1855-60.

16   Necklace, scarlet coral cameos of classical heads set in gold, *c.* 1840. Italian.

BETWEEN PAGES 64–65

17   Two Bracelets, *c.* 1850. *Above*: graduated pebbles set in silver; *below*: lava medallions with classical head cameos, set in gilt (Italian).

18   Brooch. Shell coral pastoral scene framed in gold, *c.* 1850.

19   Mosaic: Frontlet for a Comb; ruins, a butterfly and a flower-piece on the medallions, set in blue enamel and gilt. Belt Clasp; medallions of ruins set in blue enamel and gilt. Both probably Roman, of the 1830s.

20   *Pietra dura* and mosaic. *Top*: mosaic Demi-Parure, Roman ruins, *c.* 1850; *centre*: two gold Pins and a white violet Brooch set in silver, *c.* 1850–60; *right*: Pin, in gilt with mosaic flowers, *c.* 1870–80; *below*: *pietra dura* Brooch of musical instruments, *c.* 1850.

21   Mosaic and *pietra dura*. Earrings; Rome, *c.* 1860. The

Scarab, dove and lily Earrings, also the *pietra dura* Earrings, were purchased in 1870. Locket, *c.* 1870, and Brooch with mother of pearl back, probably *c.* 1850.

22 Demi-Parure of tiger claws set in gold. Indian, *c.* 1870.

23 Brooch in silver with enamels; by C. R. Ashbee, *c.* 1890.

24 Hair Bracelet with shell cameo of a bacchante, *c.* 1845–50.

25 Brooches, with miniatures of pet and wild animals and sporting subjects; all *c.* 1845–50.

26 Crosses. *Above*: two in *piqué*, made in Birmingham, *c.* 1870; *below*: gold Cross with carbuncles and pearls; in the style of John Hardman Powell.

27 Crosses. *Above*: seed pearls, *c.* 1840; silver, rustic style, *c.* 1850; gold filigree, *c.* 1850–60; *below*: coral and gold, *c.* 1860; onyx *c.* 1870; silver *c.* 1880.

28 Necklace. Crystal Collar with pendant crystal Cross, *c.* 1880.

29 Three versions of the M for Mary Brooch; by Castellani, based on a fourteenth-century design. In sapphires, emeralds and rubies, all with small rubies and pearls. All with the Castellani monogram.

30 Child's Tiara, in pink coral, *c.* 1845.

31 Parure in cut steel; made in Birmingham, *c.* 1880.

32 Earrings; in ruby red and white layered and cut glass, *c.* 1850.

Illustrations in the Text

Foreword

THE VICTORIAN period is richly various and although
sometimes an ugly period, a fascinating and rewarding era for
the collector. The collector of jewellery will find a tremendous
choice and a great range of prices, from necklaces running into
four figures at the great auctions to humble glass knick-knacks
on a junk-shop tray.

Owing to the length of the period—1837 to 1901—also the
accelerating rate of social change and rise in the standard of
living due to the Industrial Revolution, there were several very
distinct changes in mood and style. The first, the Romantic
era, owes a great deal to the Regency and the eighteenth
century and runs from 1837 through the 'forties. The eclecticism
of mood, the numerous sentimental imitations of the past,
(such as mock medieval) however, is different. The legacy lies
rather in the careful craftsmanship, the pretty choice of gems and
settings, the fattened-up Regency proportions. The watershed
between the Romantic period and the very characteristic mid-
Victorian or Grand Style (c. 1860–80) occurs at the Great
Exhibition of 1851. After this huge display of exotic imitations
and inventions in technique (including some very odd adventures
with novelty materials), a contemporary style begins to emerge.
Also a distinct development occurs—alongside the established
mode an 'artistic' style evolves—this starts with the Pre-
Raphaelites and the Arts and Crafts movement and runs into
art nouveau at the end of the reign. The Grand Style produced
some very fine jewellery, mostly imitations of the Renaissance
or the classical past, but with a gravity of design and use of fine
gems and a very conscious use of gold, that was entirely contemporary. Some of the grandest examples could be very ostentatious (Ingres's portrait of Madame Moitessier in the National
Gallery is a splendid example). This middle period is very
much an age of display and the second Empire and the English

19

Victorians across the Channel liked to shew their riches in tangible form. The most important jewellery was not however, the most expensive—for this was the time of the Castellani family and their Neo-Etruscan jewellery. Delicately made and proportioned, with an exquisite balance between gem and setting, their work takes its place amongst the masterpieces of any period. Their influence on the design of the less expensive jewellery, (as worn by the prosperous upper middle class rather than the nobility) was far reaching and entirely beneficial. The Castellani and another great Italian designer who worked in England, Carlo Giuliano, form a link between the jewellery of Victorian society and the 'artistic' or aesthetic jewellery. The last period—the Late Victorian—from 1880 to 1901 witnesses a greater difference between commercial and aesthetic style. The opening of the great diamond mines made diamonds all the rage and, in their new plenitude, they were used much more generously than before. In the last period goldsmiths' work suffers an eclipse—the gem stones, with the minimum amount of visible setting, create their own display and the diamond is the most fashionable of all. This new vulgarity is found in the most expensive jewellery and in the cheapest Birmingham paste. But the Arts and Crafts movement designers such as C. R. Ashbee, Henry Wilson and Alfred Gilbert, along with the great French *art nouveau* designers such as Lalique and Miault, and Tiffany in America, were producing at the same time most exciting jewellery, entirely new and contemporary and presaging, with a certain pioneer awkwardness, the ideas of the modern movement.

Victorian jewellery offers exciting discoveries for the collector from all periods—early, middle and late, at all ranges of price. It is beginning to be fashionable and prices are rising. But all periods produced, as no comparable times ever had before, a vast amount of ugly rubbish. The Great Exhibition catalogue shews some very ugly monsters in the numerous jewellery illustrations alongside charmingly fantastic pieces. Some rather horrid designs may make a price temporarily while the fashion lasts. Examples by good designers such as Pugin or Froment-Meurice in the Romantic period, the Castellani or Giuliano or C. R. Ashbee from the Middle and Late periods will always hold their value. For those who collect pretty trinkets at junk-shop level, there are still delightful finds to be made, although even junk-shops are becoming self-conscious and their prices are rising with their prestige.

To make finds a strong period sense is necessary, with a sharp eye and the patience to sift through tawdry rubbish until the one good piece reveals itself. The best training is constant looking at the most characteristic examples one can find and here museums are very useful. The Victoria and Albert Museum in London, both in its jewellery and costume galleries, has a great collection in the right Victorian setting. Industrial art museums where there is a particularly strong local tradition are very helpful—Birmingham has splendid Victorian jewellery, beautifully shewn close to the relevant costumes. This has important pieces as well as examples from the local industry. The Cooper Union Museum in New York has a great number of original designers' drawings as well as the jewellery itself. Both the Cooper Union and Birmingham have done Victorian exhibitions recently, with extremely useful and well-documented catalogues —the Cooper Union (1955) exhibition catalogue a model of its kind. Museums shewing costume and examples of Victoriana— Bristol (Blaise Castle Museum) and Plymouth are useful—and generally own a few examples of Victorian jewellery, which they will shew to a serious enquirer. Of country houses open to the public, Wightwick Manor just outside Wolverhampton is the most splendid example of a William Morris-Philip Webb house extant. It is not only very beautiful but in room after room there are portraits and family photographs of the Pre-Raphaelite painters and poets and their wives and children, the women wearing long chains and necklaces in the aesthetic style. Picture galleries also are useful—the Pre-Raphaelite and other

English Victorian painters in the Tate and the Victoria and Albert, Martineau, Augustus Egg, Alfred Stevens's two splendid female portraits, the portraits of Millais and Watts and Sargent's incomparable evocations of the vulgarity of the 'nineties. The Pre-Raphaelite collection at Birmingham is particularly good.

Victorian novels, particularly illustrated editions, such as the novels of R. S. Surtees illustrated by John Leech, are good guides to manners and atmosphere. The best quarry is probably *Punch* or the *Illustrated London News*, but almost any bound volume of a Victorian magazine, particularly with advertisements, is likely to prove useful. Apart from such incidental benefits, there is one book which is supremely helpful. *Victorian Jewellery* by Margaret Flower (Cassell, London, 1951) is a model guide, to which I am deeply indebted and with the aid of which I have recognized several of my best finds.

I have divided this book into topics, tracing each from the Romantic to the Grand Style and Late Victorian periods. The first is the jewellery of display, for full evening dress—the *grande toilette*, the second is the everyday jewellery worn indoors or out on informal occasions by day. Travellers' jewellery—including holiday souvenirs from nearer at hand, and the jewellery of Sentiment which follows are both especially characteristic of the Victorians and the rising standards of living which brought tourism and holidays in general within the reach of the middle class. Popular Devotional jewellery was also a peculiarly Victorian manifestation, the early crosses by Pugin important as works of art, the later crosses something sentimental, far less important, the true feeling reappearing with the *art nouveau* designers. I have included men's jewellery also—that woeful decline from the decorative male costume of the Regency to the studied anonymity of the last years of the century; and something about children's jewellery also, for in the nineteenth century children ceased to be little adults and began to have clothes and trinkets designed specially for them. And it is sometimes in the small things made in Victorian times—a child's corals, even the folk-art glass earrings of the fairground or the Birmingham toymakers' gilt work—that one finds the authentic fresh charm of the period, a simplicity that speaks for it as clearly as the designs of Castellani, Pugin or Giuliano.

Chapter One

The Grand Toilette

THE GRANDEST Victorian jewellery, that worn with one's very finest clothes, for dinner party, ball or reception, was paradoxically the most conservative in design. Although very much at the mercy of the vagaries of high fashion, there was, until the last two decades of the century, a continuity of design, even a recognizable link right back to the eighteenth century. In the last decades, however, there was a radical change.

Until the 'eighties and 'nineties, there was a certain basic similarity in full-dress fashion. At night bodices were low, skirts were wide. As hair was worn high or low, so the fashion for tiaras or jewelled combs waxed and waned. Earrings likewise depended on hair style. But the basic constituents of a parure remained the same—headdress, necklace, brooch, with a variation on emphasis. By the 'eighties, however, the silhouette was changing and by the 'nineties a new attitude to important jewellery had arrived. Pins sparkling with diamonds to be worn in the hair arrived then, also choker dog-collar necklaces, clips and buckles. In the right designer's hands the new fashions became something exciting, presaging the modern movement. Unfortunately, as far as the grandest jewellery was concerned there were many West End jewellers of good craftsmanship but boring design and only a handful of really good designers.

The grand jewellery of the first years of Victoria's reign is the most varied and charming in design and in use of materials, diamonds, emeralds, rubies, pearls and garnets, seed pearls, amethysts, all the important gem stones were used. This was the Romantic period, when young girls went to balls looking like *Les Sylphides*, in tight-waisted décolleté dresses, with vast skirts, off the shoulder fichus in lace and ribbons: a splendid opportunity to display necklaces, bracelets, brooches, earrings, headdresses, an assemblage they were expected to wear with restraint, but which their mothers wore all at once. A grand ball dress was generally satin, often white, but violet or green or other gentle shades also appeared and velvet as well as satin. The older one was the more one was inclined to colour; white with a wreath of flowers in the hair was the prerogative of the young. The 'rosebud garden of girls' was expected to 'glimmer in satin and pearls'. This was not an age in which the accent of fashion was upon the debutante. Too much jewellery was frowned upon for the young, whereas the married woman wore important jewellery to display her husband's status. The grandest of the grand jewellery was her prerogative, diamonds were for the married alone, whilst the young would have to be content with pearls. But both debutante and chaperone shared the pretty and sometimes gently fantastic styles of the Romantic movement (Frontispiece).

Jewellery was, above all, allusive. In a period when nearly every leisured lady read romantic historical novels—such as those of Sir Walter Scott—the jewellery which she wore on grand occasions reflected her favourite heroine's tastes. In evening dress after all, one could allow for a certain amount of dressing up—such as the pleasing conceit of jewelled arrows as hairpins which transfixed the elaborate coiffures of the late 'thirties. At the very beginning of Victoria's reign the *ferronière* —a sort of necklace worn on the forehead, with central jewel dangling over the hair-parting—was highly popular with evening dress. This took its name from the bandeau worn on the forehead of *la Belle Ferronière* in a portrait by Leonardo, romantically and wrongly supposed to be that of a beautiful blacksmith's wife, beloved of Francis I of France. This fashion may be traced to the Renaissance. The Gothic also inspires important

26

FIG. 1. *The Grande Toilette.* Full evening dress *c.* 1837–1900. A. 1837. B. 1845. C. 1860. D. 1876. E. 1884. F. 1894

jewellery of this first period. The *ferronière* could be worn with a tiara set back on the head behind it. The tiara particularly lent itself to the Gothic style—suave pointed arches of the early English phase, pinnacles with cusps and trefoilheads, all adorned these headdresses. Gothic jewellery was designed by Augustus Welby Pugin for Messrs Hardman of Birmingham and shewn at the Great Exhibition in 1851. This, using pearls and garnets with great delicacy, has a restraint unusual at a time when exuberance prevailed. The pearl and gold drop earrings are particularly attractive. But the great international jeweller of the period who practised the style was a Frenchman, François-Désiré Froment-Meurice (1802–55).

The stepson of Meurice, a jeweller who was himself a fine craftsman, Froment-Meurice was an original designer whose work was a very free interpretation of the Gothic. His shapes often anticipate those of *art nouveau*. His style shews rather large, heavy shapes particularly in the deep bracelets, which, carried out in gold, shewed medieval figures against an architectural frame. These bracelets were particularly popular in England.

Froment-Meurice sent jewellery from Paris to the Great Exhibition in 1851, which was much admired. Indeed, working through a Great Exhibition catalogue, one can see why. Heavier than the Pugin jewellery and perhaps not as charming, it has good if slightly massive proportions and stands out amongst the clutter of much of the English design. Rudolphi, another jeweller whose business in Paris was much favoured by the English, was less original. His work had the conservative quality possessed by much of the really grand jewellery of the period and he produced designs which owed a great deal to the eighteenth century, though heavier and more florid in their rococo settings. The diamond, ruby and emerald parure made by Lemonnière and belonging to the Queen of Spain—also shewn at the Great Exhibition—is typical of this conservative high international style (Figure 2). But although it owes much to eighteenth-century tradition, there are subtle differences. A certain solemn consciousness of grandeur, slightly parvenu, had come in with the First Empire and this was expressed in rather obtrusive settings, over-loaded detail, and the general loss of that lightness and restraint which had given eighteenth-century grand jewellery its perfection.

That same restraint also ceased to characterize the motifs used in grand jewellery. Flowers, more naturalistically treated than before, began to be popular. Two demi-parures, one of pearls, one of amethysts (*c.* 1850) in the Victoria and Albert Museum have bunches of grapes on their leaves in the necklace; two individual bunches form the earrings. The general effect is like a Dutch still-life, with its rather overloaded charm

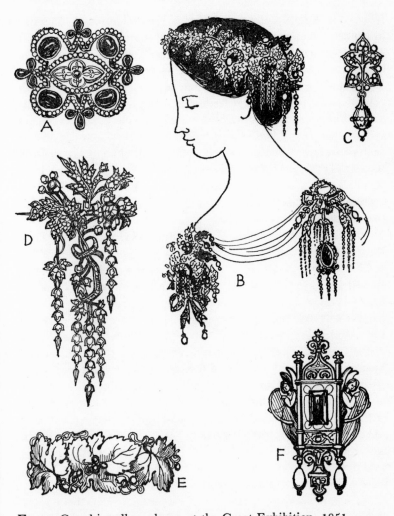

Fig. 2. Grand jewellery shewn at the Great Exhibition, 1851
A. Brooch by A. W. Pugin for Messrs Hardman of Birmingham.
B. Parure made for the Queen of Spain by Lemonnière, Paris.
C. Earring by Pugin for Hardman's. D. Brooch by Rowlands of
London. E. Brooch by Rudolphi, Paris. F. Brooch by Froment-
Meurice, Paris

(Plate 1). A less pleasing motif was the coiled snake. Popular in Roman jewellery, the archaeologizing nineteenth century had revived the snake—particularly in bracelets, but also in necklaces, even writhing, Medusa-like, in head-ornaments. Queen Victoria had a coiled snake bracelet, set with diamonds and with ruby eyes, which she wore at her first State opening of Parliament. Drawn by Wilkie in the careful sketch report he made at the time, it is a sumptuous piece of jewellery and set off her pretty forearm remarkably well. Other snake-bracelets were less successful, the entwined coils producing a confused and lumpy effect. The snake motif—although now definitely confined to bracelets and rings—appears again and again until almost the end of the reign (Figure 3).

By the time of the Great Exhibition of 1851, grand jewellery was tending towards a more careful copying of the styles of the past. By 1851, Nineveh and Babylon as discovered and popularized by Layard had been added to Napoleon's Egypt and to the marvels of Herculaneum and Pompeii as sources to copy. A French pattern-book of historic styles had come out as early as 1844. But a man who was an Etruscan enthusiast as well as a craftsman and jeweller really did most to set the style for the 'sixties. This was Fortunato Pio Castellani (1793–1865), who opened his shop in Rome in 1814. He had an obsessive interest in Etruscan jewellery, which led him to re-discover the ancient techniques of granulation and gold-filigree, which he found survived amongst the craftsmen of S. Angelo-in-Vado in Umbria. These Umbrian craftsmen he took to his Roman workshop. Fortunato Pio may have been involved in the Italian wars of liberation; it is likely that his passion for the jewellery of his country's great past was allied to an equally passionate nationalism. Be that as it may, the making of 'Italian archaeological jewellery', as he called it, ceased during the wars. His son Augusto took up the business again in 1855. His other son Alessandro, much Anglicized and a great savant, bought for the British Museum (to which he left his collection of classical

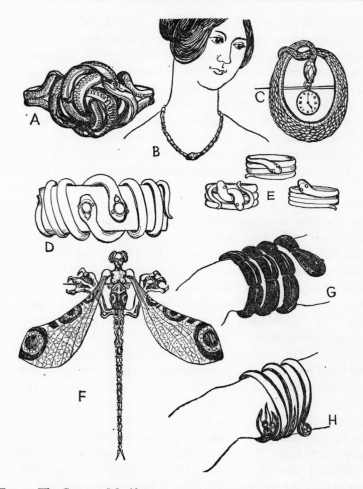

Fig. 3. The Serpent Motif: an art nouveau monster

A. Snake cluster gold Bracelet *c.*1845. B. Gold Necklace with snake clasping its tail *c.*1845. C. Gold snake Brooch with a tiny watch, Great Exhibition 1851. D. Gold Bracelet *c.*1860. E. Three Rings *c.*1875. F. Corsage ornament by Lalique, 1898. Worn by Sarah Bernhardt. G. Etruscan-style snake Bracelet in jet *c.*1870. H. Bracelet worn by Queen Alexandra (then Princess of Wales) in 1889

Greek and Etruscan jewellery) and wrote books, which were much quoted by the experts on ancient metalwork. Both with the same initials, it is difficult to disentangle the two younger Castellani. Both wrote books on jewellery, both were scholars. Augusto's collection ended up in the Capitoline Museum, of which he became Director. But it seems that Augusto was the practical designer, Alessandro the man who travelled to international exhibitions, the critic of other people's designs. Alessandro was the London branch of the firm.

This Castellani jewellery—signed with a linked C monogram (Plate 2) was of three main kinds, all of superlative quality. The modern Italian peasant style, which they conscientiously put forward at international exhibitions, was a salute to the craftsmen of S. Angelo-in-Vado, but was ahead of its time. It had little influence on English style. The second style—Neo-Renaissance—was a part of the great Second Empire vogue for elaborate jewellery. The Castellani produced jewels that the Elizabethans might have prized—an enamelled gold setting surrounding an antique cameo or an important gem stone, to be worn hanging from a necklace or chain. Several of these pendants belong to the Victoria and Albert Museum. Although highly coloured and beautifully proportioned, they have a cold perfection about them which is completely unlike the exuberance of their sixteenth-century originals. Brogden and Phillips, among the English designers, had hardly the same intuitive grasp of style, the authority or the colour sense, but they could do nearly as well. But the Neo-Etruscan style was entirely a Castellani idea and this caught on completely and, although based on gold, set the fashion for other materials as well.

It is significant that the very expensive display jewellery of the 'sixties and 'seventies was not much affected by the Neo-Etruscan style. Sir Charles Lock Eastlake's *Household Taste*—a manual, like Mrs Beeton's for the upper middle class—deplored the badness of its design: 'So long as people prefer the display of mere wealth to the encouragement of true principles in manu-

1. Two Demi-Parures, one seed pearls and gold, the other amethysts and gold, *c.* 1850. *Victoria and Albert Museum.*

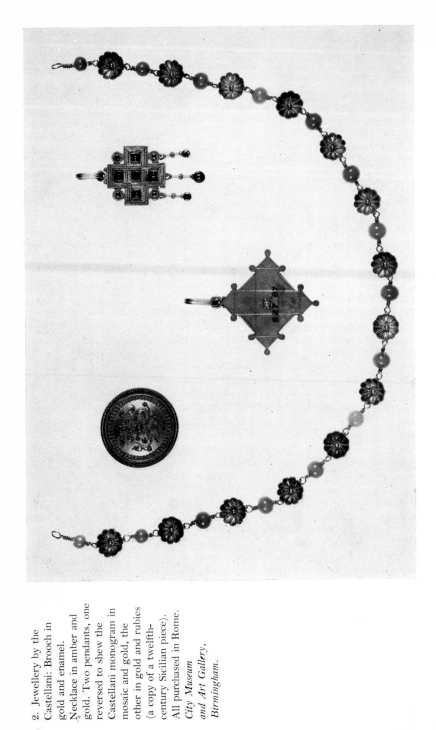

2. Jewellery by the
Castellani: Brooch in
gold and enamel.
Necklace in amber and
gold. Two pendants, one
reversed to shew the
Castellani monogram in
mosaic and gold, the
other in gold and rubies
(a copy of a twelfth-
century Sicilian piece).
All purchased in Rome.
*City Museum
and Art Gallery,
Birmingham.*

3. Bracelet. Etruscan style in gold, with a chamber for hair concealed inside, *c.* 1860.
Collection of Mrs E. M. Phillips.

4. Pendant by the Castellani signed with monogram. In gold with emerald cameo mask of Tragedy with emeralds and pearls, *c.* 1855–60. *Private collection.*

5. Necklace by the Castellani, signed with monogram. Twelve chalcedony cameos of Roman emperors with cabochon rubies and emeralds set in gold, *c.* 1860. *Private collection.*

6. Necklace in gold by Castellani. An especially fine example of archaeological jewellery, *c.* 1860. *Formerly in the collection of Martin Desmoni, Esq.*

7. Ensemble by Carlo Giuliano. In gold, with chrysoprase, rubies and pearls. Marked with the monogram 'C. and E.G.' instead of the usual 'C and A.G.', *c.* 1880. *Collection of Mr Martin J. Desmoni.*

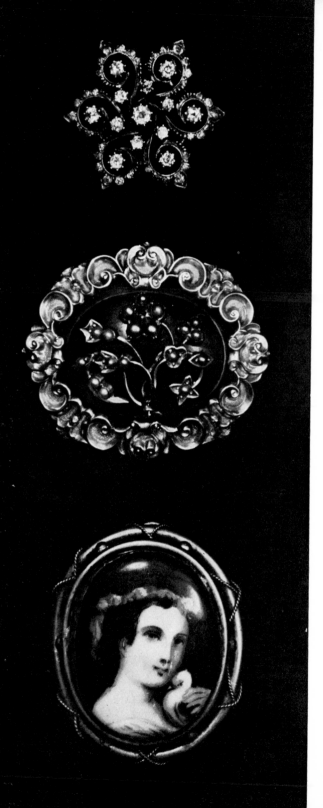

8. Three Brooches. *Top:* diamonds set in silver backed with gold, *c.* 1890; the others *c.* 1850, one pearls with dark blue enamel and gold, the other a miniature of a girl with a dove on ivory, gold mount. *Collections of Mrs Bryan Pearce and Miss Jenefer Peter.*

9. Parure, iron pyrites mounted in silver. By Goggin & Company, Dublin, 'Irish bog oak carvers to Her Majesty' (inscribed on the case), *c.* 1840. *City Museum and Art Gallery, Birmingham.*

10. Silver Locket and Chain with monogram, *c.* 1870. *Collection of Mr and Mrs Penna.*

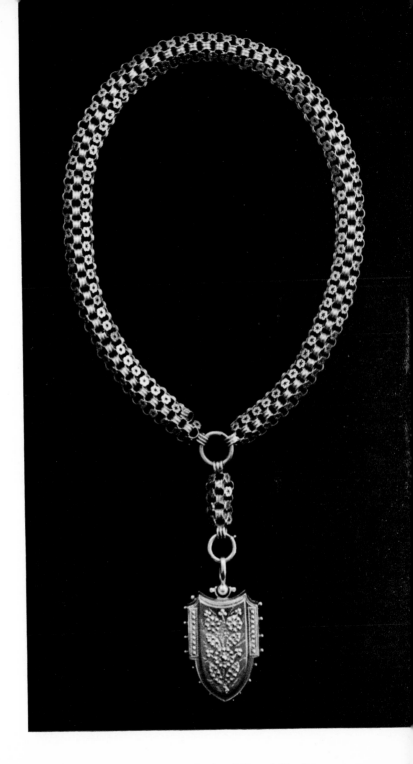

11. Silver Locket and flexible Chain, *c.* 1880. *Collection of Mr and Mrs Penna.*

12. Demi-Parure. Brooch and Earrings in ivory, *c.* 1870–80. The cross motif worked out in corn sheaves. *Collection of Mr and Mrs Penna.*

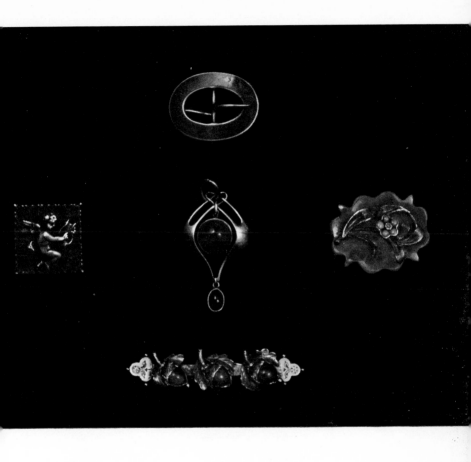

Late Victorian Brooches and a Pendant; *top* Buckle Brooch of Scottish pebble set
silver, *c*. 1890; *centre* Brooch, Cupid with lyre, malachite and silver, *c*. 1898;
pendant, gold with beryls *art nouveau* style, *c*. 1890; Brooch, soapstone with turquoise
gold flower, *c*. 1898; *below* Bar Brooch, acorns in malachite and gold, *c*. 1880.
Collections of Mrs Bryan Pearce and Miss Jenefer Peter.

14. Jet faceted Necklace and three Brooches; *above* Celtic Cross shape; *centre* with white porcelain centre; *below* faceted jet mount with crystal centre. *Collection of Mr and Mrs Penna.*

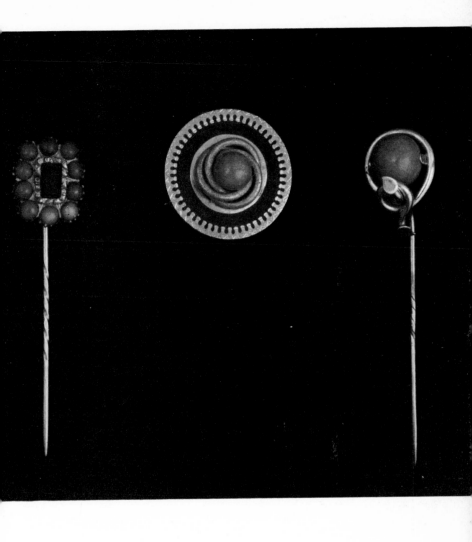

15. Coral Pins and a Brooch; *left* Stock or Tie Pin, coral, bloodstone and gold, *c.* 1850; *centre* Brooch, coral enamel and gold, *c.* 1850–60; *right* Pin, coral and gold, *c.* 1855–60. *Collection of Mr and Mrs Penna.*

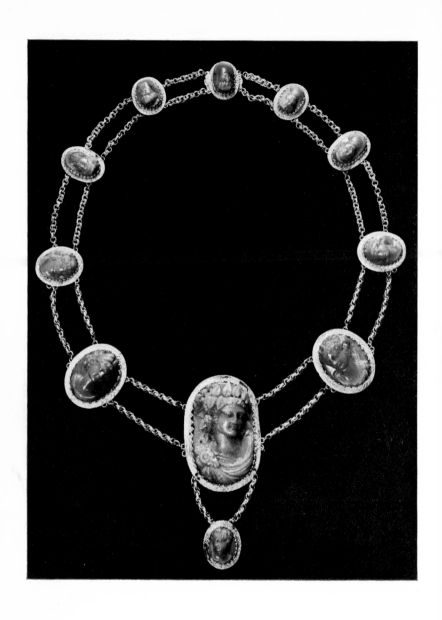

16. Necklace, scarlet coral cameos of classical heads set in gold, *c.* 1840. Italian.
De Pass Collection, Royal Institution of Cornwall, Truro.

facture, we shall work vainly for improvement in the design of expensive jewellery . . . for that exquisite school of the gold-smith's art which Castellani laboured to revive in Rome there is little popular appreciation in this country.' There was good reason for this (Plate 3). The Castellani Etruscan style used gold rather than gems, it was truly goldsmithing and the gem stones were secondary. The subtle treatment of the gold for its own sake, the play with textures—*granaglia*, filigree to decorate it, was nothing to do with display. The portrait of Madame Moitessier by Ingres in the National Gallery shews the display jewellery of the time. Camille Silvy took a photograph of the Duchess of Manchester in 1862 in which she was wearing an elaborate necklace, a brooch in the centre of her décolletage and a gold and silver belt the width of her wrist designed in a sort of Gothic openwork, like garden paling. Her earrings, dangling gold baubles, which matched a pair of gold bracelets made of the same baubles, were the only pieces which shewed the Neo-Etruscan influence.

But if the richest jewellery was over-jewelled, lumpish, the Castellani and their followers (particularly the superb Carlo Giuliano) produced jewels for more discerning patrons which would have been masterpieces in any age. The extraordinary thing is that while the Neo-Renaissance pieces are rather dead copies, the so-called 'archaeological' jewellery is not really very like ancient Etruscan: it has a quite distinct and lively spirit of its own, entirely contemporary—and this using the same tech-niques and much the same proportions. The necklaces are light —using small beads of gold and often droppers, tipped by a small gem. Bracelets are deep, like ancient amulets, and earrings share the elaboration of the classical earrings—light fidgety structures of beads and droppers and fringe, sometimes an open chariot-wheel shape. The wheel or disc and the *bulla* are used for brooches, pendants and lockets, these, in contrast to the necklaces, massive in proportion with broad golden surfaces decorated with filigree and *granaglia*, with perhaps a small central pearl or diamond. The Castellani used coloured enamel, but in small areas only, as they used gems. Alessandro had conjectured about methods of ancient Greek enamelling and having asserted its ancient pedigree, used its colour rather more freely than the ancients had done. Carlo Giuliano, whose early designs were very close to the Castellani, took the process further and used enamels even more generously. But the main characteristic of the style was the fondness for gold, gold used burnished and sometimes matt surfaced, and gold of different colours. The minute golden balls of the *granaglia* technique were molten granules soldered onto the surface, forming raised patterns which were used alternatively with filigree. The splendid bracelet of Plate 4 gives some idea of *granaglia* and filigree but its massive boldness is characteristic of the English version of the style rather than the Italian. Gold on its own—as in the necklace of scarabs at Birmingham, or of golden flowers alternating with amber beads (also at Birmingham), was used for necklaces, but these were more generally enriched with garnets, pearls (particularly freshwater pearls), rubies and enamels—all used with great delicacy. Castellani's work is shewn in Plates 2, 5, 6 and 29, and Figure 4.

Carlo Giuliano (died *c.* 1912) began with a Neo-Etruscan restraint, but his designs became more exuberant, shewing a very beautiful use of colour.

He was born in Naples, came over to England at the suggestion of Robert Phillips in the late 'sixties and set up in Piccadilly, where he and his sons Federico and Fernando carried on the business. His designs were at once less scholarly and more original than the Castellanis', with less emphasis on the goldsmith's work, more on the enamels and gems which he used to produce a shimmering effect. He designed some very light and pretty dangling Etruscan type earrings, also some very effective disc-earrings in the ancient style. These may be seen in the Victoria and Albert Museum. His pendants were especially beautiful, the shapes starting from Etruscan and Renaissance

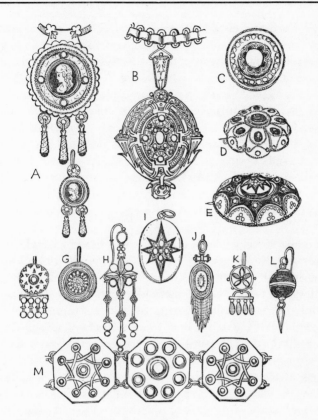

F IG. 4. Etruscan shapes *c*.1860–1870
A. Locket and earring designed by Sir Charles Lock Eastlake for the 1872 Exhibition, with red cornelian cameo, pearls and enamels on gold. B. Locket from a parure by Sir Digby Wyatt in low relief 'modelled' (*sic*) gold with pearls and diamonds (also for the 1872 Exhibition). C. Brooch by Richard Green for the 1862 Exhibition. D. and E. Two Brooches: D. gold with garnets and E. with pearls, both *c*. 1860. F. Earrings by Castellani. G. and H. by Giuliano. I. Locket with small diamonds, pearls and enamel. J. Earring by West, Dublin. K. Earring, corals and gold. L. Earring, onyx and gold. M. Bracelet, gold set with coral and turquoise (by Sir Charles Eastlake for 1872 Exhibition)

but the latest ones anticipating the freedom of *art nouveau*. Freshwater pearls, moonstones, diamonds, rubies and emeralds were all used by Giuliano with a sensibility which fully realized their beauty. His enamels, which were floated on over the gold like paint, included a slightly stark opaque white, which he used as a necessary dissonance, a contrast to his pale and liquid gem stones. An ensemble by Giuliano probably made for his wife and an important pearl and enamelled pendant are shewn in Plate 7 and Figure 5. Giuliano usually signed his work with the initials C. & A.G. The monogram mark 'C.&E.G.' on the ensemble may refer to his wife's initials. He had a pupil, Gaetano Melillo and his work is worth searching for also.

Giuliano developed beyond the Neo-Etruscan style of the 'sixties and 'seventies, in fact he is one of the links between Victorian and twentieth-century design. Meanwhile, English jewellers from eminent designers like John Brogden (influenced by Giuliano) to the Birmingham toymakers, embraced the style with enthusiasm, and varying success. Richard Green shewed some restrained and beautiful designs (brooches and bracelets), with strong simple *bulla* shapes, at the 1862 Exhibition. Other English attempts at exhibition work, notably the necklace and earrings by John Brogden shewn at the Paris Exhibition in 1867, were less successful. This set, in the Victoria and Albert Museum, is beautifully made, but where Castellani or Giuliano would be simple, this is woefully fussy. Fine cameos in chalcedony and onyx of insipid pastel colour are matched against equally insipid enamel. The result is timid and ineffective. The best examples are to be found amongst the solid bracelets (Plate 3), pendants and lockets of the simpler versions of the style. Figure 4 shews typical shapes.

It is through the champions of the Italianate jewellery, the attempt to encourage a conscious style, that the Arts and Crafts movement really begins. Eastlake, Ruskin, and later, Mrs Haweis in her *Book of Beauty* (1878), all elevated good design

Fɪɢ. 5. Pendant. Pearls and enamels on gold, *c.*1888. By Carlo
Giuliano *Collection of Mr Martin J. Desmoni*

as a positively moral quality, all deplored the jewellery of
display. Eastlake showed examples designed by himself and
by Sir Digby Wyatt (Figure 4). In the next generation the
Arts and Crafts movement designers would be making the
jewellery themselves. Eastlake had his carried out by Howell
and James. But this is the beginning of the split between
commercial and aesthetic jewellery. The Pre-Raphaelite painters

were at their height in this decade, but William Morris's influence on design had hardly been felt. The high seriousness of Ruskin and Eastlake was a beginning. The intensely professional Giuliano, with gems which were beautiful, and also costly, presaged the modern movement; the less costly designs of the artist-jewellers such as W. R. Lethaby, Gilbert, C. R. Ashbee, were to be equally important. Giuliano stood at the end of a great tradition; the Arts and Crafts designers in reaction to the commercialization which was threatening to destroy it, were beginning something new.

But in the 'sixties, although a few people might be seriously interested in the ethical problems of good design, most young ladies and their mothers merely followed the fashion. Hair was dressed more elaborately than in the 'forties and 'fifties, the emphasis being on a fullness at the back. Pearls or gold beads were twisted in the hair, perhaps with a gardenia or two instead of the wreath of flowers. As hair was worn higher ornamental combs were added. These were often jewelled, made of tortoise-shell or *piqué*. They were frequently rather ugly. The Neo-Etruscan earrings, dangling until they touched the shoulders, arrived with the fashion of hair drawn back from the ears, the earlier spaniel ringlets having disappeared. From the 'sixties to the 'eighties was the great age for dangling jewellery —pendants, lockets, chains and earrings. The aesthetic young ladies of the 'seventies wore long chains and pendants. As for the others, the 'seventies saw the Neo-Etruscan impetus dying out. Shapes grew heavier, decoration elaborate for its own sake. No gold surface was left plain, but chased or engraved with trivial all-over designs. There was a rather sick fashion for ultra-realistic birds, flowers and insects—quite important necklaces of very naturalistic bees for example and frail head ornaments of moths or butterflies, which trembled in a lifelike way. The desire for novelty had set in. But in style there was then a complete reaction.

In the last two decades, grand jewellery almost completely

changed in style. In reaction to the emphasis on gold work and
settings of the 'sixties and 'seventies, gems now became all
important, settings insignificant. Dangling earrings became
small studs or pearls; necklaces worn up high on the neck,
tight and short, veritable chokers, glistened with diamonds.
The effects of the new diamond mines were now being fully felt.
Diamonds, bare and blazing, were used in rings, shoulder clips,
aigrettes in the hair, necklaces. The modest pearl, amethysts,
even emeralds and rubies lost favour to the diamond. Young
girls now sparkled with diamond pins and brooches and diamonds in the hair. A favourite combination was that of pearls
and diamonds together. Queen Mary, photographed as Duchess
of York in 1894, has her hair set close to the head but built up
on top, a diamond pin like a stab of fire high up in the centre,
whilst the Princess of Wales, in 1889, wears two golden baubles
in her hair and one osprey plume. Queen Mary has neat studs
in her ears, a collar necklace, slender bracelets, a diamond
brooch on her corsage, whilst Queen Alexandra has a sumptuous
diamond brooch. Queen Alexandra's rather heavy corsage
brooch, with its three droppers is, however, oddly old fashioned
and suggests the style of the wedding present parure given to
her in 1863. The century ended in a blaze of pale fire, for the
colour-combinations favoured by the Castellani generation with
enamels as well as gems were now quite out, diamonds and
pearls, moonstones, opals, all shimmering, sparkling stones
were in, with occasionally a muted enamel setting.

Interior decoration, china, dresses and hairstyles reflected a
passion for the late eighteenth century and jewellery now began
to have a rather weedy Neo-Adam look. In a frail way this
could be quite pretty, as the diamond flower brooch of Plate 8
shews. Frivolous diamond dress-clips shaped like bows, diamond
stars worn in the hair, jewelled stomachers, even the ubiquitious
collar necklace or stiffened neck band, in velvet, ribbon or lace,
set with brooch, cameo or pearls, all looked back to the 1760s
for inspiration. The jewelled toys of the very rich also reflected

this taste. Fabergé set the style and his elegant trinkets looked back to the Russia of the eighteenth century.

But apart from the reproduction eighteenth-century style, some important jewellery was made in a style that was strictly contemporary and new. The artistic jewellery had at last become fashionable. It was a style which owed a great deal to the French *art nouveau,* but looked back with sympathy at the asymmetrical designs of the ancient Celtic. Looking at one of C. R. Ashbee's bold and strange brooches with their large, irregular cabochon pearls, one remembers Eastlake's pleas for texture, made twenty or so years before, for the pleasing slight irregularities of handwork, for the saving of time and precious materials wasted in order to make 'two little stones precisely like each other'. Perhaps Ashbee's masterpiece was the peacock brooch which he designed *c.* 1900 in silver and green gold with a constellation of small diamonds nearer the body, which is a very large pearl. The bird has a formidable presence, given to it by a fierce ruby eye and it struts upon a large pearl, from which an even larger pearl dropper depends. Immensely decorative, yet with an almost sinister quality, one might feel this Ashbee jewel had too much character to be entirely easy to wear. Sarah Bernhardt used to wear an even more sinister woman-headed dragonfly designed by Lalique in 1898 as a corsage ornament (Figure 3). Henry Wilson in England, Miault and Lalique in Paris, Tiffany in America were all producing similarly uncompromising designs. Giuliano, whose latest jewellery reflected the freedom of *art nouveau,* produced things which were less rugged and more wearable (Figure 6). Various other West End jewellers produced sufficiently tepid versions of the style and it was their work which sold (Figure 13 shews a compromise between the eighteenth-century style and *art nouveau*). Ashbee's moonstone necklaces in their delicate simplicity were of course infinitely wearable. But it was from the uncompromising barbaric splendours of the most fiercely *art nouveau* designs that good modern jewellery began.

Fig. 6. Necklace. Pearl collar of six strands with enamelled and pearl pendant. By Carlo Giuliano, *c.*1890. In the *art nouveau* style. *Collection of Mr Martin J. Desmoni*

The cheaper dressing-up jewellery must now be considered. Eastlake's remark in the 1860s that the less expensive jewellery tended to be better designed than the really grand is true throughout the whole Victorian period until the commercialization of the last decades, for the jewels that the middle-class ladies decked themselves out in for their parties, balls and routs, were frequently more imaginative in materials and texture than those of their richer sisters. In the early Romantic period, a parure of seed pearls or coral was frequently prettier than a glittering array of diamonds. This is a pleasant fact for the small collector, for whom the pompous arrays of important gems are quite out of price range.

A parure of coloured blown glass prettily shaped and neatly set in gold; green enamels or malachite instead of emeralds, can be quite as attractive as an important set made of the most precious gems. It is in these cheaper sets that the most ingenious and fantastic designs of the Romantic movement are to be found. Experiments with new techniques and novel materials were also made with these cheaper pieces, there was a great use of flexible gold chain, for instance, in both necklaces and bracelets. A complete parure in iron pyrites, mounted in silver in a design of Irish harps and shamrocks made by Messrs Goggin of Grafton Street, Dublin, 'bog oak carvers to the Queen', about 1840, has a fantastic charm (Plate 9). Brooches and earrings made of coral hands, set in golden lace cuffs, could seem a little surrealistic and a tiara of branched coral must have made the wearer look like a sea-king's daughter; but earrings which were ivory jonquils or roses, accompanying a flowery necklace and a brooch have the same kind of charm as have early Victorian flowerprints. Bold brooches using a large semi-precious stone set in an elaborate border of golden flowers were effective with their clear colour and the naive florid setting. The keynote of the less expensive Romantic jewellery is a certain floridity. Everything is ample, generously proportioned; brooches tend to be oval, worn horizontally. Bracelets, too, with stones set in flowery gold settings are deep and strongly made. Necklaces, neither choker nor pendant, sit beautifully to the neck and are better than those of the later periods at flattering an opulent bosom and shoulders. A decep-

Fɪɢ. 7. Necklace and Pendant, Pin, Comb and Brooch. All by Henry
Wilson, *c*.1896. The Pin in silver, the Comb in silver, the gems
probably pearls and acquamarines, the Brooch aquamarine and
enamels in silver. The Necklace silver with pearls

tively simple graduated coral necklace of three strands of round
beads gathered into a paste clasp came alive when worn, lying
just right to the neck and having this subtly flattering quality.
This coral necklace was all that remained of a parure.

A complete parure is hard to find, and expensive when found.
Of the next period, the Mid-Victorian, the most easily found
dress jewels are the ubiquitous pendants, brooches, lockets and
bracelets. The form of these secondary pieces of jewellery
deteriorated during the 'seventies and 'eighties, even more
than did that of the more expensive jewellery, as they became

heavier and clumsier, and thin and fussy chasing and engraving of the gold and silver began to take the place of gems. Bracelets began to look like napkin rings, so deep were they, often hinged and often diapered all over with some thin and meaningless pattern (engraved forms of bluebells for example), but better when they had raised patterns such as the ornamental pillars which made a hefty all over pattern on a bracelet in a catalogue of 1885. There was also the expansion of a cheap manufactured jewellery trade, centred on Birmingham. The toymakers of Birmingham had been making metal buttons, buckles and trinkets since the eighteenth century. This led to the appearance of jewellery that was badly made as well as weedily designed. The fantasy of early Victorian Romantic jewellery was replaced by a sort of coy jauntiness. This started off with the Japanese taste of the 'seventies—which quickly degenerated from Whistler's aestheticism to tea-shop Japanese. By the 'nineties when the mass-produced jewellery had sloughed off its heavy and elaborate settings in favour of something thinner, cheaper and flashier, coy pairs of lovebirds in paste were fluttering on thin gold bracelets, and lucky clover leaves and hearts, also in diamonds or paste decorated bracelets, brooches and rings. The inept obviousness of the design of this cheaper dress jewellery is irritating, the shapes are not thought out in terms of their material, they are at once too naturalistic and too artificial. Henry Wilson, the craftsman-designer in his *Silverwork and Jewellery* (1902) was thinking of contemporary commercial designing when he wrote 'all the natural forms should be generalized. In your studies be as minute as you please . . . but when you translate these studies into work, learn to leave out. The artist . . . seeks forms typical of his subject and yet suitable to his material.'

Arts and Crafts Guild designers such as Henry Wilson were in fact a blessing to the more aesthetic middle-class ladies of the 'nineties. For here was jewellery that did not depend on costly gems for its effect. It strove against 'exaggerated elegance and an endeavour to suggest ideas of luxury' which Wilson found 'enervating and repulsive'. It was an attempt to use gold and silver and stones in a way which would bring out the natural beauty of the material. Some of these designs look mannered, crabbed and contorted to us today; they lack the soaring professional craftsmanship of a Giuliano for instance. But using cabochon pearls, moonstones, garnets and amethysts sometimes with enamel and set in various coloured gold and silver, sometimes even in pewter, they often had a modest beauty.

Wilson's book describes modest jewellery designed at last according to principle. It is functional. 'Necklaces should be designed on a circle of $4\frac{1}{2}''$ diameter and all pendants should be arranged on radial lines,' he said and: 'No pendants should go beyond the semicircle or they will hang awkwardly on the shoulder when worn.' Figure 7 shews some of his designs—the lucid, well proportioned necklace a simple contrast to the almost baroque quality of the hair ornaments, and the very mannered pendant. His *art nouveau* curves were never too languid, they are a bit too close to Celtic ornament for that, and he did try not to copy the ancient styles, only to be influenced by the best of them. He told his readers to look at Egyptian, Mycenaean, Etruscan, Anglo-Saxon (odd that he does not mention the Celtic when it is so clearly a personal influence) but said, 'Do not attempt to copy . . . study the principles of contrasted line, texture and form.' 'Design,' he said, 'is the expression of your personality in terms of the material in which you work.'

There are some rather skimpy little relics of late nineteenth-century dress jewellery to be collected that are either reproduction eighteenth century or watered down *art nouveau*, pieces which are pretty in a thin sort of way. Beside the sturdy designs of the craftsmen jewellers they look rather inadequate. But silver filigree pins and bows for the hair, stiffened neck 'collarettes' sewn with seed pearls, even meek little turquoise-flowered brooches and corsage ornaments have a certain nostalgic charm.

45

Chapter Two

Everyday Jewellery

VICTORIAN upper-class and middle-class women, as their standard of living rose, became creatures of infinite leisure. This meant a social life with very definite rules and formalities. The period was stiff with rules of etiquette, which in the last decades at least were kept evolving by the middle-class fashion magazines and female domestic journalism. From Mrs Beeton onwards there were many encyclopedias of household management which dealt with the conduct of social life, as well as the command of a household. A certain amount of dressing up was involved. And the jewellery appropriate was naturally rather different from that worn for dress occasions at night.

In the early decades little jewellery was worn by day. Brooches, rings, belt buckles, the occasional belt or girdle, or long neck chain; earrings were worn, when the fashion for ringlets did not render them superfluous, but worn sparsely. The full ruffled cuffs of the day clothes of the 'forties obscured bracelets. Necklaces and bracelets appeared mostly at night only. By the 'fifties bracelets appeared with everyday clothes, worn in pairs and quite often over gloves. The brooch or locket at the neck became ubiquitous. Rings continued to be popular throughout the period. In the 'sixties the brooch yielded a little to the locket and chain, but quite often brooch, locket and chain were worn all at once. As the neckline of everyday and outdoor clothes became high, almost military—in the 'seventies and 'eighties—in its severity, so the brooch became more essential. In the last decade there were a host of ornamental hat-pins and tiepins and women began to wear ornamental pocket watches on light chains. Now too, sporting jewellery began to appear.

The most obvious everyday jewellery to be worn throughout the period was the ring. The everyday rings of the early Romantic period are delightful. They were generally flowery in inspiration—pearl flowers with tiny diamond centres set in engraved and pierced shoulders, enamelled pansies or forget-me-nots, or flowers carved in coral set in gold, or large single gems set in rococo floral gold settings. There were also concen-

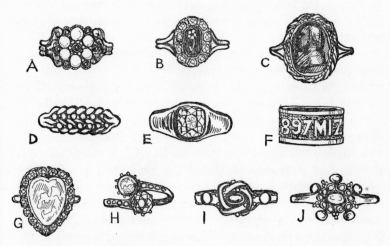

FIG. 8. Rings from 1837 to 1900
A. Central ruby, pearls and turquoises in gold, *c*.1845. B. Diamond and enamel on gold, 1845. C. Head of Charles Dickens in scarlet coral with gold, *c*.1850. D. Gold plaited ring, *c*.1880. E. Man's Ring, diamond, gipsy-set in a ring made of two wedding rings, *c*.1876. F. *Mizpah*, man's gold Ring commemorating thirteen years of a friendship, 1897. G. Heart-shaped opal surrounded with diamonds set in gold, *c*.1890. H. Opal and diamond cross over in gold with seed pearls set in the shoulder, *c*.1890. I. and J. by Henry Wilson, both garnets or opals set in silver

tric circles of small stones—turquoise or seed pearl or coral with a small diamond in the centre. Pearls, garnets, turquoise, diamonds and emeralds were the favourite stones, sometimes enamel was used but this material only came into its own later on. Pearls were much in favour in engagement rings. On the whole rings tended to be light and simple, but there were some eccentricities—the ubiquitous coiled serpent appeared as a ring, with ruby eyes. And then there were the rings in the Gothic taste; Pugin designed some pretty ones in gold and enamels with pearls, and Froment-Meurice, although his were nearer the great rings of the Middle Ages, cumbrous, with groups of figures on the bezel. The rings of this early period differ from those of the 'sixties and 'seventies in the proportion of gem setting: although small stones were often used, they were grouped together to form a flowerhead for instance and the setting itself, although often carved and pierced, was relatively unimportant. In the Mid-Victorian period however settings became heavy, emphasized—a solid band of gold might be decorated with three smallish star-set diamonds or with a string of tiny stones set all round in diamond-shaped panels. Plain gold was chased and engraved; the conceit of a buckled belt was popular (set with enamel, these) and the serpents writhed in ever-thicker coils. A new design was the gipsy setting, in which the stone was set flush with the gold. Figure 8 shews a quite important diamond gipsy-set, with the thick gold band reducing the importance of the gem. Single large gems, claw-set in the conventional way, likewise had much thicker shoulders than before. In this period rings began to drop in price and it was possible to purchase a simple gold one—without gems of course —for under a pound. At the other end of the scale were the rings designed by Giuliano, Renaissance in influence and using large gem stones in a rather conservative way, with a lightly propor-tioned gold mount, often pierced and generally enamelled. A deceptively simple looking, and very beautiful, Giuliano sapphire ring set in enamelled gold may be seen at the Victoria and

Albert Museum. These Giuliano rings make the English everyday rings of the period look thick and heavy.

But in the 'nineties the revulsion felt for the earlier, heavier designs produced weediness in all kinds of commercial jewellery. This shewed particularly in the rings. The diamonds and rubies flash prettily, but it is almost as if the enterprising jewellers had tried to produce the ugliest possible settings for them. The nastiest are the two and three part rings and the cross-overs. The two and three part rings were ingeniously made of thin flattened bands of gold, supporting closely disposed clusters of gems (mostly diamonds and pearls together). The cross-over was a weedy little band of gold with open ends each terminating in a stone. The cross-over survives as a design today, but hearts and the true-lovers' knots—perhaps two (pearl) hearts conjoined surmounted by a diamond cluster knot—have largely disappeared. The prettiest rings of this period were the simplest —the gold circlet with five small pearls and coral gipsy-set in it and sold for £2 in its day, or the rope-like arrangement of fifteen little pearls flanked by two single ones, known as the Turban pattern, retailing at £1 7s 6d.

The rings made by the artist-craftsmen for the aesthetic ladies in this last period have a touch of Froment-Meurice about them. If the commercial jewellery is skimpy, this tends to be unwieldy. Henry Wilson's design for a gold ring with emerald, ruby and pearls was somewhat heavy and confused, and his filigree table-ring of silver, set with garnet, opal or chrysoprase of almost barbaric heaviness, but his simple knot ring of silver set with garnet, opal or chrysoprase is very decorative. Figure 8 shews the table-ring and the simple silver knot.

If rings were worn throughout the period during the day, during the Early Victorian era, very little other jewellery is visible out of doors and not much indoors in daytime save for the more stately, social occasions. A photograph of Miss Elizabeth Rigby, later Lady Eastlake, taken in 1844 shews her hair wound up into two thin birds' nests in front of her ears, from a sleeked dutch doll's centre parting, and pinned into her hair are a pair of single pearls. She wears rings and a long, fine chain and no other jewellery is visible. The fashion plates of the time shew little jewellery. A photograph of a rather frail looking young woman taken in 1849 shews her in a quite elaborate bonnet, with long broad flowery ribbons and a dark coloured walking dress, with a large brooch of what looks like topaz pinned at the bosom of her dress. A long gold chain also shews, and rings on both her hands. But apart from the occasional modest brooch, it was not until the 'fifties and 'sixties that much jewellery was worn by day on informal occasions. After that brooches, earrings and bracelets were worn as a matter of course and more and more of them until the masculine-cut outdoor clothes of the 'nineties made their use, at least out of doors, unsuitable. Gradually informal daytime jewellery began to acquire a character of its own.

Bracelets were worn at night over long evening gloves. Now (in the 'sixties and 'seventies) they occasionally appear over gloves with outdoor costume when ladies are visiting. They

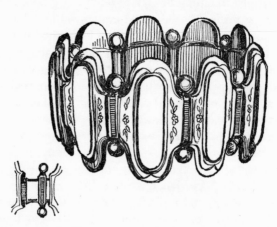

Fɪɢ. 9. Bracelet in the Etruscan taste. In brass, *c*.1860. Each segment threaded with flat elastic

were worn within the house, of course, with afternoon dress. The simplest kind were of metal, unjewelled, with segments, strung like beads on elastic. Figure 9 shews one, about 1860. Simpler variants of full dress jewellery were worn, flexible gold chain, with tiny links arranged to let it move with the smoothness of a snake, plain or engraved deep gold bands and, the beginning of a fashion which still exists today, the curb chain of gold links, sometimes with a chain or little golden heart dangling from it. Gold bracelets counterfeiting a strap or garter with a large buckle upon it were also popular during the 'sixties and 'seventies. A thinner version of the Etruscan shapes persisted as bracelets, became narrower, lighter (Figure 10).

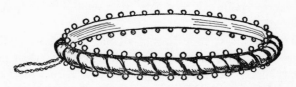

FIG. 10. Bracelet. In gold, *c.*1875. *Collection of Mrs Philip Williams*

In the late 'eighties and 'nineties increasingly practical and severe, rather mannish, tailored suits led to the eclipse of daytime bracelets, save with formal afternoon *at home* dress, or to be worn with the dubious 'tea gown' which came in at the end of the century. Perhaps then a narrow sporting bracelet, of thinnest gold decorated with a diamond horse-shoe or hunting whip might be allowed to declare the owner's tastes.

Brooches, lockets and chains, shared the same fate as the bracelets. From the 'sixties, until the late 'eighties, large brooches finished off the high neckline of day dresses, sometimes with a locket and chain dangling gracefully just below. In the early 'eighties pendant and locket and chain finished off the narrow rectangular décolletage of some afternoon dresses. Rather heavy, lumpish necklaces, often of crystal, amber or jet fulfilled the same function. A crystal necklace of this style is shewn in Plate 28. Long strings of pearls were worn in conjunction with velvet or lace boned collarettes or a dog-collar necklace in the 'nineties. *Art nouveau* chains and pendants, or trailing necklaces of amber were worn by the ladies of the aesthetic movement.

Although not as immediately appealing as early Victorian jewellery, these everyday sturdy gold or silver chains and lockets of the 'sixties and 'seventies are nicely made and pleasant to wear. They are also much more reasonable in price than earlier necklaces. Two are shewn in Plates 10 and 11 dating from between 1870 and 1880. Their rather weedy engraved decoration and the weak shouldered shape of the lockets spoils them. But the chains are beautifully engineered.

Perhaps the most appealing of all the everyday jewellery of Victoria's reign are, however, the earrings. From 1837 to 1850 long earrings were the fashion, although between 1840 and 1850, ringlets rather obliterated earrings in any case. In 1850 the hair styles allowed the ears to be seen once more and the neat, small earrings came back. But by the 'sixties and 'seventies drop earrings had returned, so long that they tangled with bonnet strings. Dangling earrings gave way to small studs or pearls in the ear or none at all in the 'nineties and then Princess Mary gave the long earring a renewed popularity and, at the very end of the reign, long and short earrings were both in fashion. Few earrings of the first Romantic period of the Victorian style are to be found, save amongst the elaborate evening jewellery. But from 1850 onwards earrings were worn not only at home, but outdoors, especially as small pill-box or fez shaped hats were now as fashionable as the all-enveloping bonnet. Informal earrings developed one shape which was mostly used for day wear only. This was the *Creole*—a half moon, often wide at the ends. It is to be found in all sorts of materials: human hair plaited very finely into a woven mesh and mounted in gold or pinchbeck was very popular early in the period but went out of fashion in the 'seventies; jet was also used (*see* Figure 21) and coral. The *Creole* was a variant on another informal shape, the hoop. As well as gold a thin hoop of coral was frequently used. Earrings occur in all the rather eccentric materials described in the chapter on Traveller's Jewellery but for everyday wear gold or gilt was popular, particularly in the Neo-Etruscan fashions of the 'sixties when round or elongated gold baubles, many with tassels, hung in

FIG. 11. Everyday Dress from the 'forties to the 'nineties
A. *c.* 1845. B. *c.* 1855. C. *c.* 1860. D. 'Aesthetic' costume *c.* 1870.
E. *c.* 1883. F. *c.* 1896 (outdoor). G. *c.* 1896 (indoor).

heavy drops from the ears. The delicate working of the gold, with the *granaglia* and gold wire so popular at this time, was most successful in these earrings. In the middle 'sixties the earrings became an important part of the general ensemble of the coiffure; earrings and hair-comb were often designed to match for afternoon wear. Jet or *piqué* were often used for such a set. By the later 'seventies the desire for novelty had rather spoiled many of the shapes and what had been charming metal working had now become over-fussy engraving. Also a truly dreadful desire for the inappropriate began to manifest itself— birds in their nests, coy little monkeys, beetles, flies, ladders, croquet mallets, Tyrolean hats and sabots were all made into gold earrings. Horse-shoes and saddles were to be worn when riding. Occasionally such conceits as ivy-leaves, cockleshells, acorns or bells might be pretty, particularly when the earrings were small and neat in shape. By the 'eighties the small earring was definitely in favour again, discs (often with Etruscan ornament), daisies, clover-leaves, pine-cones appeared, all little and neat. One really good idea was a ball of gold, which closed around a solitaire diamond for wear during the day. Small gold coins now began to be mounted as earrings. Gold was not the only material for eccentric shapes; coral and ivory were used as well. An ivory demi-parure of *c.* 1870 with earrings in the form of sheaves and a cross pendant to match is shewn in Plate 12.

By the 'nineties earrings were much less popular during the day. The severe mannish style of the tailor-mades worn then, topped by a boater or a mock-homburg, made them look very incongruous. Stud-earrings screwed in the ear were the newest thing; a discreet pearl stud might be worn in the afternoons, leaving the diamonds to flash at night. By 1897 however, very small modest drop earrings were fashionable again and at the very end of Victoria's reign, more varied shapes were in fashion, all however, small and light compared with the earlier ones. They look thin and timid against the splendidly fantastic droppers of the 'sixties.

The same development from bold simple shapes to rather small and timid ones, may be seen in the brooches which Victorian ladies wore by day. Less sumptuous than full dress ones, they were often more eccentric in design. They tend to grow in size and importance until the 'seventies and then they dwindle, in scale and significance of design, until they end as the mean bar-brooches of the 'nineties, almost entirely depending

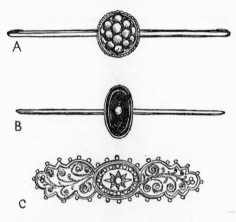

Fig. 12. Three Bar Brooches:
A. Turquoise, *c.*1870. B. Onyx with seed pearl, *c.*1890. C. Gold with seed pearls, c.1880. All in gold. C. Is very typical of its period, but of better quality than usual.
Collection of Miss Josephine Harris

on their gems for character, with little interest in the setting (Figure 12). Brooches and buckles by the artist jewellers in the 'nineties were so different in style that they underline the immense gap dividing commercial and artistic production.

Under her chin and right in the centre of her high-fastened collar the lady of the 'fifties wore a large important brooch, usually either oval or round in shape. This focal point in female costume carried on when high plain necks and tightly buttoned bodices arrived in the 'seventies and 'eighties. Where there was décolletage (occasionally in the lace ruffled afternoon dresses of the late 'eighties) the brooch became a pendant, or was mounted on a velvet neckband or collarette. Large brooches were worn at the neck of riding habits until the 'nineties. There was an enormous range of material to choose from in the earlier brooches. By the 'nineties however this had settled down to simple gold or silver or alloys, mostly mounted with pearls or small diamonds or both, or moonstones, onyx, turquoise, opal or amethyst, on the whole rather pale coloured stones.

Fig. 13. Pendant, *c*.1890. In silver with diamonds, peridots and spinel. *Collection of Mrs Philip Williams*

Even if the brooch ended rather palely, it started with great variety and flamboyance. Ladies wore brooches of bouquets made of parian (unglazed porcelain) or *Belleek* (with a high rather pearly white glaze) porcelain or with a miniature painted in enamels or a landscape embroidered in hair. The exotic materials for brooches brought back from abroad will be elaborated upon in the next chapter. There were as well brooches made of gem stones and enamels, brooches of jet with gold stars or a small pearl set in them and brooches of onyx. Settings started by being elaborate: from what looked like interlaced branches in gold, to plaited ropes of gold or the vaguely nautical looking border of the brooch with an enamelled miniature on it in Plate 8. But settings and shapes became more simple, brooches larger and of bolder form—mainly round or oval. About 1880 the bar-brooch began to appear. An early and very pretty example set in gold, with malachite acorns amongst leaves is shewn in Plate 13. The bar-brooch, so much lighter and more unassuming than the great solid *bulla* shape of the 'sixties and 'seventies, gradually took its place. At the same time, the more conventional brooch diminished in size. Three of the later type of small neat brooch, perhaps dating from *c*. 1870–80 and all made of jet, are shewn in Plate 14, with a contemporary jet necklace. Bar-brooches could be mass-produced with ease by the jewellery firms of Birmingham and exported to the London jewellers for sale, with girls' names engraved on them, or mottoes, or sentimental family inscriptions such as 'Mother' or 'Pet'. Slightly more expensive brooches with diamond horse-shoes for strictly sporting wear (brooches with golf clubs also came out) marked the discovery of diamonds in South Africa in the late 'sixties; from then on the diamond became a much less exclusive jewel. The discreet bar-brooches, worn when visiting or at afternoon tea, often had a row of small stones, little diamonds or three moonstones or onyx set the same way.

From 1860 to about 1880 a locket or pendant on a chain accompanied the brooch. The pendants and brooches often have much the same shape or design, in fact some brooches were designed to be worn as pendants as well. Lockets also share the same shapes but are more often oval than round. The large, solid convex shape of the brooch had only to be deepened a little to allow for the locket's contents. Often a brooch had a concealed compartment in its back. In fashionable jewellery the locket or pendant-and-chain motif almost disappeared after the 'eighties, but the aesthetic ladies who wore the jewellery made by the Arts and Crafts movement designers continued to wear them. Some flamboyant *art nouveau* pendants appeared, notably by the French jeweller Miault of Paris. C. R. Ashbee and Henry Wilson also designed rugged pendants, Miault used gold set with rubies, but in Paris *art nouveau* was high fashion. A few decorous small pendants of near *art nouveau* design were made in England. One in gold and beryls appears in Plate 13. This minor jewellery is pleasant enough, but timid in design.

One item of everyday jewellery remains to be mentioned. Victorian ladies loved long, fine, useful chains. In the daguerrotypes of the 'forties otherwise jewel-less ladies hold eyeglasses depending from a chain which stretches from neck to waist. A chain could hold a seal, a watch, a reticule. In the 'seventies the Benoiton chain (so-called after a dashingly fashionable French family in a play) hung from the bonnet to the waist. In the 'nineties the rich wore immensely long pearl necklaces, below the pearl collar. Beads or the ubiquitous chain took their place amongst the less prosperous. A photograph taken in 1901, Queen Victoria's last year, shews four ladies in outdoor summer dress, each one of them wears a chain or long knotted necklace, two are wearing short collar necklaces also.

Yet another useful item which is eminently worth collecting is the hat or bonnet pin and its ally, the more frivolous female version of the tiepin. Bonnet pins, mainly in silver or gold filigree, were worn between 1840 and 1860 and when small hats began to be fashionable alongside bonnets in the 1860s they had to be stabbed into place. It would be possible to make an interesting collection of pins alone, for in a simple miniature way they shew the main changes in jewellery design from the 'forties to the end of the century. They are generally substantial enough to be worn in lieu of a small brooch today. They are also very reasonable in price. Two small coral pins are shewn in Plate 15, both early; the one on the left may be, in fact, a cravat pin. The substantial one on the right is of very good quality. *Pietra dura* or mosaic pins as shewn in Plate 20 are also attractive. Some of the pins of the 'nineties were of much poorer quality; a vast variety came from the Birmingham jewellers, in very eccentric shapes in gold, silver or various alloys decorated with small pearls or diamond chips. Often enamelled, they took the form of Japanese fans, helmeted heads, the crescent moon, conch shells. The neater tie- or lace-pin, decorated with a sporting device such as a horse-shoe, sometimes has a certain weedy charm.

Chapter Three

Travellers' Jewellery

IF THE Georgians were the people of the grand tour, the Victorians could almost be said to have invented the holiday abroad. In search of romantic scenery they crammed themselves into coaches and in conditions of great discomfort, often braving banditti, drove over mountain passes to reach Florence, Rome, Naples, Pompeii and Herculaneum, even far away Attica. On these marathon excursions, they sought tangible evidence of their travels, hence the tourist jewellery: mosaics, cameos, corals, the bland Hellenistic faces carved in shell, mother-of-pearl, onyx, volcanic lava or basaltes. There was also the jewellery from farther afield: soldiers, sailors, members of John Company posted to India and the Far East bringing back tiger-claw parures, ivory lockets and filigree necklaces in soft matt silver or gold for their wives and sweethearts. Lastly there is the travellers' jewellery near at hand—the holiday souvenirs from the British Isles themselves: Celtic brooches from Ireland, cairngorms set in silver from Scotland and all the geological jewellery coming from different regions of England to remind people of industrious geologizing holidays.

The cameo is the type of tourist jewellery most often to be found today. The cameo, set in different sizes and ways, remained popular from the earliest years of Victoria's reign until almost the very end, although the etiolated examples of the last decades were rarely high fashion. The earliest are by far the best, compact in design, beautifully made, with a proper feeling for texture. The tremendous burst of chivalrous feeling for Greece,

60

lately liberated from the Turkish domination, with which Victoria's reign began, made the schoolroom classics come alive in a new and romantic way. Steel engravings of Lord Byron abounded. The Maid of Athens was celebrated by amateur sopranos in many Victorian drawing rooms. Cameos made in Paris and in Italy, particularly in Florence and Rome, expressed the fashion. The Castellani designed sumptuous necklaces with cameos, using gem stones of great quality (Plates 4 and 5). One of the chief makers during the 'forties and 'fifties was Isler of Rome, working mainly in onyx, sometimes in coral. A very fine necklace dating from this period, with coral heads in high relief, comes from the de Pass Collection in the Royal Institution of Cornwall. A large head and shoulders, of Bacchus probably, for the head is wreathed and garlanded with grapes, is flanked by two smaller female heads, Demeter and Artemis (Plate 16). The elaborate cameo earrings also in coral from the same collection are much later, probably dating from the 'seventies (Figure 14). They are examples of the most sumptuous kind of travellers' toy—the souvenirs of the rich. Indeed, some fine parures in the early period were carried out in gold and cameos. The subjects of cameos were mostly taken from Greek mythology: a cameo of Endymion confronts Artemis on one necklace and, in an oval brooch of *c.* 1870, Athena drives a chariot (Figure 21). Occasionally, specifically Italian subjects appear—Roman matrons, veiled in the toga, or Homer and Virgil confronting Petrarch and Dante, as in the laurelled heads carried out in volcanic lava on a bracelet. Another bracelet, in pinchbeck, with Roman heads in lava medallions graded in colour from almost pure white through drabs, buffs and greys to milk chocolate brown is shewn on Plate 17. This dates from *c.* 1850. Bacchus—perhaps because of his curling vine-wreaths—and his maenads also, were favourite subjects from beginning to end of the period (cf. Plate 24). Rather indeterminate, vapid nymphs' heads also abound. Occasionally medieval subjects appear. A certain type, linear in quality and oddly like Millais' drawings of the 'forties, is probably English. These, made in shell, have a delicate, fresh quality which is very charming. An early cameo of a different type, probably English, is shewn in Plate 18; it shares the same naive charm. The same rustic subject but without the lamb also exists. Some English jewellers set out deliberately to vie with the continental makers. Messrs. Phillips shewed a very elaborate oval brooch in the Great Exhibition, a laurel-crowned female head in cameo, set within bands of deep blue enamel filled with a sort of crazy paving of small diamonds, the whole topped with an eagle in diamonds. Sir Charles Lock Eastlake's

FIG. 14. Earring. In scarlet coral, very finely carved. Italian, *c.*1870. *De Pass Collection, Royal Institution of Cornwall, Truro*

designs, in red cornelian and gold, for a cameo, locket and ear-rings for the 1872 International Exhibition (*see* Figure 4) share the same tentative character. The locket, enriched by pearls and enamel work, is rather heavy, the earrings simpler and nearer the Italian in style.

Eastlake's plea for good proportion comes over more strongly in his writings than in his designs, which are often pedantic and fussy. Unfortunately, his admonitions were largely ignored by a generation who confused ostentation with good taste. Very large oval cameo brooches, set in ponderous gold, became the fashion, but that the large brooch could be decorous and well designed was shewn by the exceptionally restrained and beautiful examples made and shewn by Richard Green at the 1862 Inter-national Exhibition. These, however, were exceptions as were the cameo pendants, really Italian Renaissance pastiche, designed by the great Giuliano about 1875. An onyx portrait cameo pendant set in enamelled gold, rubies and pearls by Giuliano, now in the Victoria and Albert Museum, is an important piece of the jewellery of the *haut monde*, very different in style from the ordinary shell or semi-precious cameo. Cameos towards the end of the century deteriorated. By the frivolous 'eighties they were no longer high fashion, but they survived as tourists' pieces, becoming more and more stereotyped and glassy look-ing. The cameo lingered on in stud earrings and droppers. Some jet drop earrings of the 'seventies, with pale cameo heads, are unusually attractive, with the effect of a silhouette in reverse.

Second only to the cameo in importance, as tourist jewellery, were the products of the Italian mosaic workers. This mosaic jewellery was made in Florence, Rome and further south. In the North around Florence a type known as *pietra dura*, with com-paratively large pieces of coloured stone, was made. The true mosaic of minute tesserae came from Naples and the South. The vogue did not last as long as that for the cameo: the most characteristic examples are found no later than the early 'seventies. As usual, the earliest mosaic pieces are the best, some degenerate late ones having tiny narrow slivers of stone as tesserae, producing a rather pale and bitty effect. The pin with a bunch of flowers on it in Plate 20 is an example, also the rather weedy earrings of Plate 21.

The mosaic technique was a descendant of ancient classical mosaic on a tiny scale—hence its fascination for the tourist. Minute pieces of coloured stone and marble were cemented onto a flat surface to produce views of classical temples, birds, beasts and flowers—even some classical figure subjects. No very large unit was made of this mosaic: the largest things are the brooches and bracelets and belt clasps, and these, circular or oval, are rarely more than 1½ inches in diameter. Brooches, necklaces of linked rounds or ovals, stud or drop earrings, hat- and tie-pins are most usual. Occasionally a tiara like the one at Birmingham shewn in Plate 19 was made, but this dates from the early exuberance of the Romantic period, not later than the 1830s. *Pietra dura* lent itself to larger pieces than the southern mosaic. Mrs Flower illustrates a splendid parure of it set in gold, *c.* 1845. This has very simple blush pink roses against a black marble background, one branch of rose to a medallion, a gold frame around ornamented with appliqué vine leaves. There are drop earrings with smaller sprays on the drop, the round at the top decorated with one tiny rose, larger stud earrings with a spray each and a round bracelet of great opulence with two full blown roses and their buds, each delicately graded from a deeper pink in the heart of the flower to palest pink at the petal's edge. The marble of the leaves is varied in the same minute way, from a light golden green to dark grey green. The blush-white rose bud on the gold-mounted pin in Plate 20 and the earring in Plate 21 shew the same technique more modestly. Parures of such grandeur are rare, much of the early *pietra dura* or mosaic work being set in pinchbeck or gilt; in the 'fifties and 'sixties, however, gold or silver settings—a large plain band— are usual with a black marble border next to the mosaic. Single flowers are often found mounted in the heavier settings

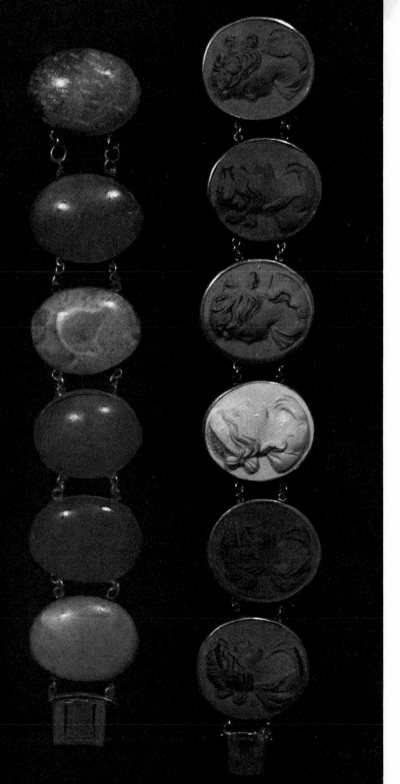

17. Two Bracelets, *c.* 1850; *above* graduated pebbles set in silver; *below* lava 'medallions' in colours from off-white, drab and donkey grey to light red, all with classical heads set in gilt. *Collections of Mr and Mrs Penna and the Author.*

18. Brooch. With large shell coral pastoral scene framed in gold, *c.* 1850. *Collection of Mrs Kingerley.*

19. Mosaic: Frontlet for a comb, with ruins, a butterfly and a flower piece on the medallions, all set in blue enamel and gilt; Belt Clasp, Medallions of ruins set in blue enamel and gilt. Both probably from Rome, 1830s. *City Museum and Art Gallery, Birmingham.*

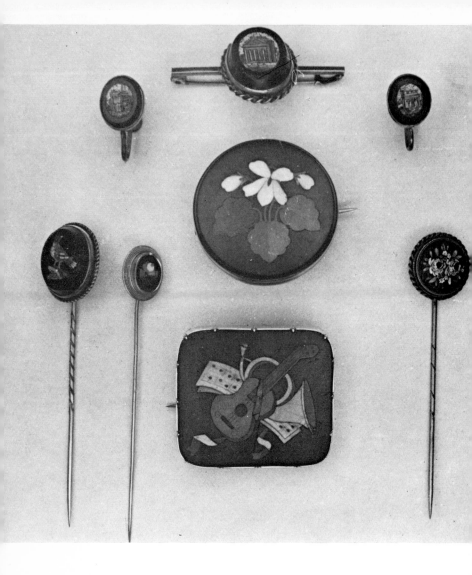

20. *Pietra dura* and mosaic; *top* mosaic Demi-parure with Roman ruins set in black enamels and gold, *c.* 1850; *centre* two gold pins and a Brooch with white violet (*pietra dura*) set in silver, *c.* 1850–60; *right* pin, in gilt, mosaic flowers, *c.* 1870–80; *below pietra dura* Brooch with a trophy of musical instruments, *c.* 1850. *Collections of Mrs Philip Varcoe and Miss Jenefer Peter.*

1. Mosaic and *pietra dura: top and centre right* Earrings, the classical head design taken from a Pompeian fresco, said to have been purchased by a Mr Archer, surgeon of Edgbaston, in Rome, *c.* 1860; the *scarab, dove* and *lily* Earrings, also the *pietra dura rosebud* Earrings were purchased by the Museum in 1870; *centre left* Locket, *c.* 1870; *bottom right* Brooch (with mother of pearl back), probably *c.* 1850. *City Museum and Art Gallery, Birmingham.*

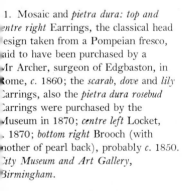

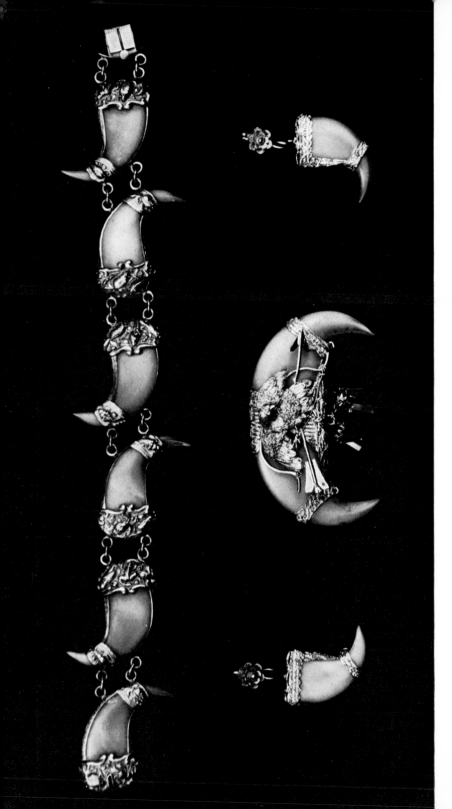

22. Demi-parure of tiger claws set in gold. Indian, c. 1870, with original ivory case, red velvet lining. *Collection of Miss Child.*

23. Brooch, silver, with enamels by C. R. Ashbee, *c.* 1890. *Victoria and Albert Museum.*

24. Bracelet, plaited brown hair and shell cameo of a bacchante set in a rococo gold frame, *c.* 1845–50. *City Museum and Art Gallery, Birmingham*.

25. Brooches. A set of miniatures framed in gold of sporting subjects, pet and wild animals All c. 1845–50.
Victoria and Albert Museum.

26. Crosses; *above* two in pique, made in Birmingham, *c.* 1870; *bottom right* gold cross with carbuncles and pearls. In the style of John Hardman Powell: purchased from an exhibition held in 1886, this looks earlier in date. *City Museum and Art Gallery, Birmingham.*

27. Crosses; *above* seed pearls, *c.* 1840; silver, rustic style, *c.* 1850; gold filigree, *c.* 1850–60; *below* coral and gold, *c.* 1860; onyx, *c.* 1870; silver, *c.* 1880. *Collection of Mr and Mrs Penna.*

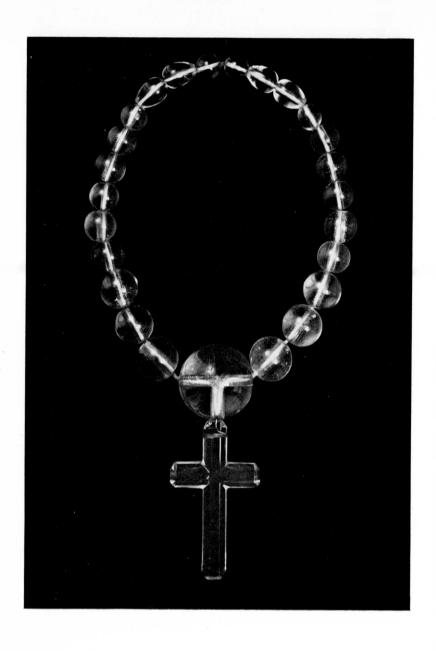

28. Necklace. Crystal collar with pendant crystal cross, *c.* 1880. *Collection of Mrs Philip Vascoe.*

29. Three versions of the M for Mary Brooch. By the Castellani, based on a fourteenth century design. In sapphires, emeralds and rubies, all with small rubies and pearls. All with the Castellani monogram. These brooches are almost exactly like the brooch (probably 1360) left by William de Wykeham to New College, Oxford, in 1404. *Private Collection.*

30. Child's tiara in pink coral, *c.* 1845. *City Museum and Art Gallery, Birmingham.*

31. Parure. In cut
steel. Made in
Birmingham, c.
1880. *City Museum
and Art Gallery,
Birmingham.*

32. Earrings. In ruby red and white layered and cut glass, *c.* 1850. *Collection of Miss Jenefer Peter.*

of the 'sixties, Plate 20 shews a round brooch of a white violet and two buds against a black marble background set direct onto a plain silver band, typical, in its plainness, of the time. The flowers in *pietra dura* and mosaic are always, incidentally, the flowers of the classics—roses, pinks, narcissi, violets. By the 'sixties the fashion for the charming but rather nursery birds and beasts of the earlier period had died away, mastiffs with flannel-pink tongues, engaging birds on branches were no longer popular. The Medusa heads of Plate 21 are rather different: a direct link with the classical past. These might have been souvenirs for those dusty full skirted lady tourists and their husbands, to be seen in a group photograph of 1868, being conducted round the ruins of Pompeii by Thomas Cook himself.

The classical views shewn on mosaic jewellery would have the same appeal. A complete parure, coloured the true dusty apricot pink, of broken Roman columns, shewed a set of views of Rome, including St. Peter's and various picturesque bridges as well as the Colosseum, Pantheon and Temple of Vesta. Larger views occupied the medallions of the necklace, small temples close up made the earrings and two of the most majestic prospects appeared on a pair of bracelet clasps. The whole was bordered in blue enamel and set in gold. This was made *c.* 1840, but the fashion persisted. Simpler and later examples, a small brooch and a pair of earrings banded in black and mounted in gold, appear on Plate 20. The rectangular *pietra dura* brooch in the same illustration, a trophy of musical instruments, is an unusual and very fine example, although the mount is missing. Its style suggests the 'sixties.

Most of the mosaic to be found today is of comparatively modest value—and always was. Such jewellers as Biancini of Florence, however, produced tourist jewellery for the very rich. In the 'sixties he made flashy, but very skilful *pietra dura* flower pieces, set in fine goldsmiths' work employing the fashionable Etruscan graining. Such costly prettiness was well beyond the middle-class tourist market and *pietra dura* of this quality is beyond the price range of the small collector today. Most of the examples illustrated, however, were picked up for very small prices.

Another jewellery material much beloved by the tourist in Italy was coral. The skeletal remains of coral polyp colonies living in the warm Mediterranean, it was cut and polished by hand mainly at Torre del Greco, near Naples. Some was exported to be made up by foreign jewellers, such as Robert Phillips of Cockspur Street, who actually received a decoration from the King of Italy in 1870 for his work in developing the Naples coral trade. A great deal was actually made into tourist jewellery in Naples or Genoa and its popularity lasted throughout the period. Again, it was a material used equally for very grand jewellery, especially in the years when it was high fashion —from 1837 until about 1867—and for very simple things: a child's coral beads, modest rings and pins—until the end of the century. The most prized was the darkest colour, but the gentler-toned pink coral was also popular, especially for young girls' jewellery in the 'forties and 'fifties. It was carved into cameos. Plate 16 shews it used for cameos, Plate 30 for a child's tiara, Plate 15 for pins and a brooch, or more simply into bunches of flowers for brooches, single flowers for earrings. It was even worn in its original branched shape, as extraordinary parures in the London Museum and at Birmingham shew. The central brooch of Plate 15, with its boss shape and the twisted gold nest in which the coral is mounted, suggests the 1860s. Among the rings in Figure 8 is a coral cameo of Charles Dickens, probably made late in the 'fifties. But one of the best Victorian corals for modern use is the necklace of coral beads. Occasionally, beautifully worked and graded coral necklaces do turn up, at remarkably reasonable prices.

Much less sophisticated design came from further afield. This was more particularly travellers' jewellery than tourists'. The growth of British influence is reflected in the Indian, Near and Far Eastern jewellery which officers of the East India Company, sea captains and naval officers brought back to their wives and sweethearts. Occasionally Near Eastern jewellery turns up, which has an engaging simplicity of style, such as a Turkish silver necklace and earrings, the necklace with grained clasps set with turquoise, made *c.* 1837. Unfortunately, the desire to please a foreign market sometimes had sad results on design— hybrid jewellery which was neither good European nor Oriental in style. Materials were often highly exotic. Tiger-claw jewellery made in India is an example. Tiger-claw earrings and brooches set in gold or silver filigree are most often found. Illustrated (Plate 22) is a demi-parure, of superb workmanship, made specially for one of its owner's ancestors and still kept in its original ivory box lined with crimson velvet. The filigree here is gold. In the same collection is a brooch made of petrified fish scales (skate) and seed pearls, set in gold and thoughtfully provided with an extra skate scale in case one should fall out. This, despite the curiosity of its material, is very pretty

Fig. 15. Bar Brooch. Petrified skate scales and seed pearls set in gold, *c.* 1880. *Collection of Miss Child*

(Figure 15). Some Indian jewellery and particularly the filigree, was over-fussy and attenuated, some, much admired by Sir Charles Lock Eastlake for its bold irregularity, preserved a certain sturdiness of proportion and taste in matching of gem to setting, which English work had lost by the time *Household Taste* was written. But this Rajput jewellery, examples of which

Sir Charles saw in the Victoria and Albert collections, was not the kind of thing normally brought home by the traveller.

Much more usual were intricately detailed ivory bouquets carved out in ovals to be brought home as lockets, or the silver-

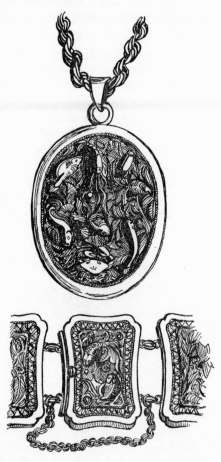

Fig. 16. Locket and Chain and Bracelet, oriental silver with fish and crab decoration. Not a pair, but with very similar decoration. *Collection of Miss Child* (*Bracelet*)

work from China and Japan. This was also imported by Liberty's from the 'eighties onward and was part of the craze for the Oriental which affected the aesthetic movement. Illustrated in Figure 16 is a locket and chain and a bracelet of silver medallions of this type, owned by different families but carrying almost exactly identical decoration. Unpretentious pieces of silver turn up quite frequently in the bargain trays of antique shops. Fashionable among the artistic young ladies of the 'eighties and 'nineties, although they lack the glamour of sterling silver, they have a soft patina of their own and are not out of place with modern clothes. Their design shares some of the qualities of *art nouveau*, upon which it had an influence.

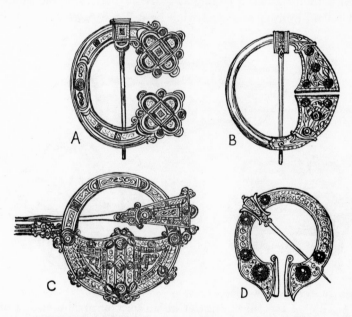

FIG. 17. Celtic Jewellery: A. and B. and C. Brooches after ancient Celtic designs shewn by Waterhouse of Dublin at the Great Exhibition. C. is a replica of the *Brooch of Tara*. D. Brooch by Howell & James, exhibited in 1862

Another most potent influence on *art nouveau* had its beginnings in what was at first a tourist or holiday fashion for regional jewellery. This was the Celtic style. Celtic jewellery of the thoroughgoing Irish kind turned up first as a proudly Irish contribution to the Great Exhibition, when several Irish jewellers, especially Messrs Waterhouse of Dublin shewed replicas of ancient pieces (including the famous brooch of Tara, with its sophisticated curvilinear decoration) and some very dubious free adaptations of ancient designs. In the 1862 Exhibition, Richard Green among his chastely designed neoclassical brooches, shewed a boss of gold strapwork formed into a Celtic crosshead and Howell & James shewed a design nearer the original in feeling (Figure 17). In 1878 Alessandro Castellani himself observed what he called a *Scottish* school of

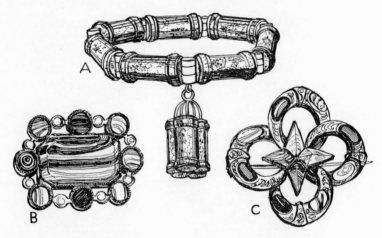

FIG. 18. Scottish Jewellery:
A. Granite and silver Bracelet in 'a choice of granite made from Aberdeen, Balmoral, etc.' by Messrs Rettie of Aberdeen. Shewn at the Great Exhibition 1851. B. Cairngorm Brooch set in silver, *c*.1850. C. Scottish Pebble Brooch in various colours and silver, *c*.1860. *B and C from the Collection of Mrs Philip Williams*

design in English jewellery, inspired by the traditional designs of the Anglo-Saxons and Celts. In its most ordinary aspect, this meant cairngorms (a brownish smoked quartz) or Scottish pebbles mounted in a boss or open circle—shaped as brooches, mostly in silver or silver gilt, which were immensely popular souvenirs of the fashion set by the Queen, for all things Scottish (*see* Figure 18, Plate 13). These brooches, sometimes gently attractive with their muted peaty colours, sometimes clumsily plain, were once very easy to find and very cheap. They have recently become much more difficult. The conscientious and clumsy replicas of the Irish jewellery, however, directed attention to the originals, and designers went to look at the Victoria and Albert Museum and the British Museum. By 1902 when *Silverwork and Jewellery* by the *art nouveau* designer Henry Wilson came out, the examples of good design chosen for illustration were Anglo-Saxon, Celtic and early medieval originals and the student was particularly directed to study early jewellery in the British Museum and at South Kensington. C. R. Ashbee's designs and Wilson's own shew the influence of Celtic, assimilated and completely understood. Some of the beaten copper, silver and pewter belt buckles, clasps and brooches by amateur workers in the craft which were made in the 'nineties shew less understanding. They are now the pathetic dross of junk-shops. C. R. Ashbee's *Ship* brooch in the Victoria and Albert Museum (Plate 23) shews the dangers of the style.

If Celtic brooches, Irish bog oak brooches and Scottish pebbles fascinated the holiday-tourist at home, there were other regional souvenirs hardly less popular. One long-lasting Victorian enthusiasm was the Geological holiday. A charming Dicky Doyle drawing of the 'sixties shews young ladies with vast skirts and neat workmanlike hats, attacking seaside cliffs with geological hammers. Blue John or Derbyshire fluor-spar with its deep marbled blue made delightful rings. This was the great period of the Cornish tin and copper mines. Rare mineral specimens were eagerly collected, malachite, amethyst and other decorative quartz, and garnets all were to be found in Cornwall. Fossils were made up into jewellery—little curled up ammonites found near Whitby dangled as earrings. A modest bracelet of polished pebbles set in silver, changing in colour from tabby grey through to earth-red and olive green, in Plate 17, shews this type of jewellery at its best. It is frequently engaging, sometimes even quietly beautiful, but hardly ever expensive to acquire. It was never high fashion (the Scottish craze was too widespread for that) but its best specimens come from the earlier periods. In late Victorian times, people were less enthusiastic about learned holidays, their souvenirs much more tawdry.

Chapter Four

The Jewellery of Sentiment

THE VICTORIANS during all the phases of the Queen's long
reign were deeply attached to sentimental symbolism. They had
a desire to commemorate the deaths of loved ones, even pet
animals. Elaborate mourning jewellery was worn all through
the reign. Perhaps the cholera and typhoid epidemics, the
prevalence of tuberculosis, wars like the Crimean, large families
in which one or two children often died young, encouraged this
preoccupation. Certainly the Queen's long years in widow's
weeds helped the attitude. But the jewellery of sentiment also
commemorated romantic attachments, engagements, weddings,
even business partnerships.

Early in the reign the jewellery of sentiment was at its most
inventive and charming. This was the great period of hair
jewellery, a tangible keepsake of the beloved, sometimes a
pathetic reminder. Hair was plaited into bracelets, half moon
shaped *Creole* earrings. Arranged in decorative patterns it filled
lockets, made up into rather wintry looking brown bouquets it
was used for brooches. Most usually, plaited into a pattern and
bordered neatly with black enamel, it filled the place of a gem
stone in a mourning ring. Some of this work was professional,
but a great deal was done by amateurs. One could buy kits of
the necessary equipment and as the makers pointed out, it was
much safer to do one's own hair-work as otherwise one could
not be sure of getting the right hair back, thus completely losing
the point of the operation. The easiest way of mounting hair was
to buy a gold ring, already decorated with black enamel, with

a hair box concealed in the bezel. Some of these enamelled rings, decorated with forget-me-nots on a heart-shaped bezel are very pretty. The black and gold colour scheme was also often relieved by seed pearls. On brooches and lockets there was more room to set off plaited hair bordered in seed pearls—for example a rectangular gold brooch with a neatly plaited central motif of golden brown hair, surrounded by an enamelled border with memorial inscription in gold gothic lettering on black substantially framed in seed pearls. Another, more modest but charming paste brooch with blond plaited hair is shewn in Figure 19. Lockets, in black enamel with golden forget-me-nots

Fig. 19. Brooch. Paste set in gilt with a centre of blond plaited hair, *c*.1840. *Collection of Miss Jenefer Peter*

set with seed pearls, opened to reveal a lock either fanned out like a plume, or screwed into an elaborate curl, and a memorial inscription. Sometimes the lockets contained a miniature instead of hair, later the ubiquitous photograph—indeed an unwieldy ring *c*. 1860 even has a tiny photograph set in seed pearls on the bezel instead of hair. Inscriptions in enamel are simple—mostly confined to *In Memoriam* with initials or name, and date of death.

Hair continued to be popular for mourning jewellery until the end of the period, but its time of high fashion belongs to the early, Romantic phase. By the 'seventies it was considered bad form in society, unless concealed in a locket etc. from sight (cf. Bracelet with hair-chamber, Plate 3). Tiepins of coiled hair mounted in twists of gold were popular in the 'nineties and Birmingham turned out cheap lockets with black enamelled *In Memoriam* inscriptions and plenty of room for a lock of hair inside, but all this is cheap stuff. It bears no comparison with the sleek plaited bracelets of the 1850s (Plate 24) or the late, but beautifully made watch fob of hair given by a sea-captain's wife to her husband in 1886 (Figure 23), or the superbly vulgar brooch and pendant of *c.* 1854, of black and gold enamel embedding a central gold-mounted crystal, under which the hair is spread out like Prince of Wales feathers, another crystal dangling from it with a small curl arranged in an elaborate ringlet. Hair embalmed in crystal like a fly in amber, or set against enamel, black or blue, has a certain morbid charm. But jet, which followed it in the later years, has an even stronger fascination. The simple, large shapes of jet jewellery, dictated by the material, make it very wearable today. It has a faceted black shine, like patent leather in shoes, which has even a certain gaiety. It looks splendid against clean, bright colours.

Jet, found at Whitby, is a sort of shale related to coal. It was known in prehistoric times (a Bronze Age jet button, buried with its owner and so clearly a prized possession, is preserved in the Art Gallery at Plymouth) but only worked extensively from about 1800. It had a short period of immense popularity when the Court went into mourning for William IV. In 1853 a trade worth about £20,000 a year seemed prosperous enough. By 1870 it was worth £84,000 and 200 workshops were engaged in it. The death of the Prince Consort had brought about this tremendous increase. The only jewellery permitted at Court was made of jet. Marie Mallet, going to the widowed Queen as a young maid-in-waiting described the custom with gentle bitterness.

The fashion that started so sadly at Court, gradually gained a

Fɪɢ. 20. Locket. In jet, inscribed 'In Memoriam' on front, the back engraved with flowers, the whole of exceptionally fine craftsmanship. *Collection of Doctor Donald Towle MD*

much more general currency. The great singer Adelina Patti had her photograph taken clashing with jet in 1867, and her fondness for it stimulated the demand, at least amongst the middle classes. Jet amongst the aristocracy was at times a Court custom but never a prized possession; although there were eccentric exceptions such as the pendant of chiselled gold and jet set in imitation of a Norman jewel in black diamonds (*c.* 1868) and the parure of dogs' heads carved in coral set in jet, which was considered particularly suitable for country house wear in 1869. On the whole the great parures were not designed in jet, but in the 'sixties and 'seventies lockets, bracelets, necklaces, earrings, pendants and combs and head ornaments delighted the middle range of society. The material lent itself well to the buxom shapes, the heaviness of prevailing designs. Today the locket shewn in Figure 20, which is of exceptional quality in its craftsmanship may have rather too strong a character, but a long, prettily faceted bead necklace as in Plate 14 is cheap to acquire and easy to wear. Delightful too are the simple jet bracelets, in lozenges, ovals or diamonds of jet, all threaded close together (Figures 21 and 22). As early as 1857, the Misses Lutwidge, aunts of Lewis Carroll, were photographed by him playing chess together, each wearing a pair of bracelets over her cuffs, of close-threaded jet ovals. Jet *Creole* earrings or simple drops or faceted balls are also very attractive (Figure 21).

In the period of its great popularity, jet was often combined with other materials. From the design point of view, this is less successful, although a jet frame to a cameo (Figure 21) may be pleasing. A bar brooch with blue forget-me-not set in jet was

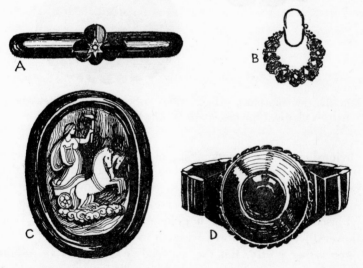

Fig. 21. Everyday Jewellery in Jet:
A. Bar Brooch with gold star and pearl. B. Creole Earring. *Both collection of Miss Child.* C. Cameo Brooch in grey shell set in jet. *Collection of Mrs Charles Girling.* D. Etruscan Bracelet. *Collection of Miss Jenefer Peter.* All *c.*1860

FIG. 22. Jet Bracelets. All c.1860–70. Segmented and strung on narrow elastic. *Collection of Mr & Mrs Penna*

obviously intended as a mourning piece, but the blue is quenched by the black and makes the whole thing funereal rather than pretty. Jet and ivory combined together are sometimes successful, sometimes too baldly black and white. Jet frames to mosaic, jet used as a setting for a gold star or for gold and ivory flowers, jet and pinchbeck were all more suitable together and often rather pretty. But the material is at its best as Adelina Patti wore it, with great polished jet balls for earrings, a chain of jet with a locket, big simple shapes which brought out the character of the material.

Jet was so popular that an imitation—'French Jet' in black glass—was brought out. This has an entirely different character and texture, much sharper facets and a different shine. It is also very attractive and very cheap.

Fashions changed in the 'eighties and 'nineties. The more finicking shapes of jewellery, the importance of gem rather than setting, made jet less fashionable. Jet fringes still glistened on black dresses, long jet necklaces, rather weedier than heretofore, were still worn. But the vigorous rather heavy shapes which favoured jet were out. It was worn for mourning still, but skimpy bar brooches with engraved inscriptions made in Birmingham silver, and equally vapid little lockets with faint fernlike shapes engraved on them for decoration and inside a faded, doll-like photograph, sometimes hand-tinted, took their place.

In the earliest Romantic period, jet had occasionally been used to frame a memorial miniature. The fashion of miniatures worn as jewellery went back to the Hilliard lockets and the portrait jewels of Queen Elizabeth's time—the Drake miniature by Hilliard is an example. But the Elizabethans, although exuberant, never carried the fashion as far as Queen Victoria. In the 'forties she owned a gold-mounted bracelet with miniature portraits of all her children. Her subjects followed suit, portrait brooches were fashionable, or if one had no portrait, at least a romantic lady on ivory (Plate 8 shews an example) in an open-work gold frame. People wore the portraits of their favourite dogs, terriers or hounds on brooches—the Victoria and Albert Museum owns a complete set, framed up together (Plate 25). These romantic extravagances were less characteristic of the 'sixties and 'seventies, when the miniature portrait tended to become a photograph and disappeared discreetly, inside a locket, but in the last period there was a vogue, started in Court circles, for pendants with insipidly coloured photographs, sometimes set with small diamonds, or plainly in gold. These are interesting perhaps as period pieces, are beautifully made and modestly simple, but not particularly attractive.

The jewellery of sentiment was at its most whimsical when

it conveyed feelings of attachment. Here again, the Romantic period was full of invention. The simplest form of symbolism is to be seen in the 'Regard' ring, where gem stones pick out the word—Ruby, Emerald, Garnet, Amethyst, Diamond. In the same way the word 'Dearest' could be made. Smallish stones set in pretty rococo settings of gold make these rings very charming, also rather expensive to acquire. The device of clasped hands appears wistfully on rings, earrings and brooches sometimes fashioned in gold or more often in enamels framed in gold, but such conceits more or less died out in the more sober 'sixties and 'seventies. The true-lovers' knot framing a heart on a 'ribbon' of flexible silver shewn in Figure 23 is late in date, but exceptional in its charm and fantasy. Engagement rings were, between 1840 and 1860, mostly pearl half-hoops, modest and pretty. In the last period, diamonds became permissible in an engagement ring. At the very end, in 1900, a catalogue lists diamond and pearl cross-overs at seventeen pounds and a 'Fine Pearl and Diamond double heart and knot' could be had for seventeen pounds ten shillings. But this was ostentatious rather than pretty, the stones standing out from their insignificant gold settings in too dominant a way, the shapes—hearts, ribbon-bow, over-fussy. The jewellery of affection in the last period was sadly commercialized, the symbolism too obvious. Fine stones were used in vulgar designs—cooing doves on a diamond brooch, joined hearts popular on diamond brooches as well as rings. A charming conceit from the end of the period is the bracelet in gold formed of the loosely linked letters of the girl's name. The cheaper mass produced jewellery abounded in name brooches—a bar-brooch, sometimes fussy, sometimes mercifully plain, engraved with 'Mother' or 'Alice' or whatever the girl's name was, mostly carried out in silver. These little brooches, rather pathetically, crowd the junk-trays of antique shops. Occasionally they have a certain charm. A circular silver one, dedicated to 'Mary' is unusually pretty (Figure 23). The fashion of wearing a regimental badge as a brooch dates from

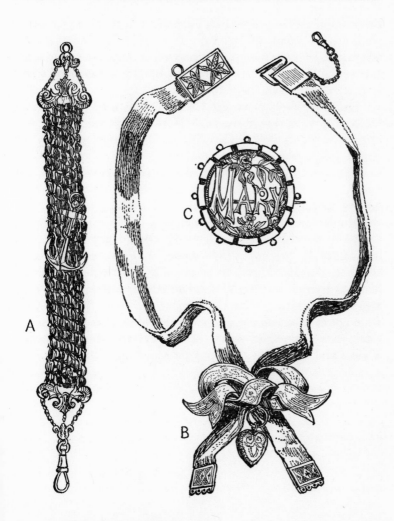

Fig. 23. Sentimental Jewellery:
  A. Watch fob in bright brown woven hair and gold mounts.
Inscribed on back *Janie to Alfred* 1886. B. Flexible silver 'ribbon'
necklace with True Lover's Knot and small silver heart, *c.*1880.
C. Name brooch in silver, *c.*1890. *Collection of Miss Child*

the wars of the last period of Victoria's reign. These brooches were always small, worn on the lapel of the rather masculine tailored suits of the period and ranged from the beautifully made diamond specimens of the rich to the humble enamel and silver or gilt badge replica made in Birmingham.

Wedding rings, of course, were simply made of different kinds of gold during the period. In the early years they were often worn with an Eternity ring, a plain hoop generally set with a single line of small stones.

The early rings might be of chased and engraved gold, the middle period saw a strong solid ring and in the last years they became rather narrower—sharing the prevailing fashion.

Commemorative rings were not only worn in mourning, or to celebrate romantic attachments. Often they cemented a friendship. A ring of 1897—dated, and engraved MIZPAH round its outside (Figure 8) is one of a pair exchanged by two business partners—friends, who had started a firm at that time and whose names are inscribed inside the ring. MIZPAH rings were not at all uncommon, rubbing shoulders in the commercial catalogues of the last decade of the era with the sentimental devices and designs of the more showy engagement rings.

Chapter Five

Special Categories of Jewellery

A VERY special type of jewellery peculiar in England to the Victorian age was devotional jewellery, particularly the cross. Since the Reformation English lay people had worn little jewellery that was specifically Christian. Now in Victoria's reign, with the great spiritual revival of the Oxford Movement, the return to the Catholicity of Anglicanism and the re-establishment of the Roman Catholic hierarchy, things began to change. Portraits of Christina Rossetti dating from the 1840s shew her wearing a small jewelled cross at her neck and devout English ladies began to wear crosses as pendants. These crosses were mostly inspired by early Gothic. The catalogue of the Great Exhibition shews some of these early designs, from the free and very romantic use of medieval motifs by Froment-Meurice to the precise and beautiful use of Early English by Pugin. Augustus Welby Pugin (1812–52) was architect and engraver as well as designer. He was a devout Roman Catholic and inspired by the slender purity of early Gothic, in which he recognized a devotional sensibility close to his own. His exercises in Gothic, such as the Houses of Parliament, preserve something of Regency proportion and, like the style which inspired them, have an oddly two dimensional effect, like a delicate drawing. Pugin's delicacy and sense of scale appear in his jewellery designs, which are amongst the finest of the time. These ranged from strictly ecclesiastical pieces, such as the crozier designed for the Bishop of Lincoln, to small crosses to be worn as pendants from a necklace. The drawing for the crozier shews a spareness and austerity not at all characteristic of early Victorian design. As Waterhouse said, Pugin's drawing 'was but a diagram to show with clearness but without elaboration what the craftsman would need and nothing more'. The small crosses, designed between 1844 and 1850, have the same lightness and a simple use of gems, such as small pearls and rubies set in gold, which is entirely successful. These were designed for Hardman of Birmingham, a firm with whom Pugin had a long connection, and shewn by them at the Great Exhibition. Birmingham City Art Gallery owns a beautiful cross in gold and enamels probably by John Hardman Powell (1827–95), a pupil of Pugin whom he succeeded in 1852 as chief designer to Hardman's and who married Pugin's daughter. This is a typical example of the style (Plate 26).

Much more easy to find than crosses by Pugin or his school, which hold their own with the great foreign designs as works of art, are the sentimental little crosses turned out in great numbers in the 'fifties—tree-trunk crosses wreathed in ivy or looped with flowers and made mostly in ivory, although they appear in other materials, notably a rather soapy pink coral. These rustic crosses vary greatly in quality. Mrs Flower illustrates an unusually fine one, in ivory, accompanied by elaborate earrings of birds carved upon a bough. In their design, these artless pieces reflect the influences which produced the oleographs hung in cottage parlours of distraught maidens clinging to great rugged crosses upon rocks, with waves almost engulfing them. Plate 27 shews examples, also two Italianate crosses of the 'sixties. Typical of the 'seventies is the slightly weedy little corn sheaf cross of Plate 12. The same weediness, a certain weakness of shape, shews itself in the two *piqué* crosses made by the Birmingham jewellers some time in the 'seventies (Plate 26). The *piqué* technique—originally introduced by Huguenot craftsmen in the seventeenth century—used tortoiseshell inlaid with silver and gold. In the 'sixties it became popular for the cheaper jewellery. It made pretty earrings, brooches and buttons and in the 'seventies was mass produced in Birmingham, the cross pendant being especially favoured. Some of the finest crosses of the 'sixties and 'seventies were made in the Italian tradition, the important English jewellers preferring to copy rather than to originate. Mrs Haweis in *A Book of Beauty* (1878) noted an elegant cross, copied from a picture by Quentin Matsys in the National Gallery, at Messrs Phillips of Cockspur Street. Mrs Haweis attempted to justify this timidity by pointing out that the English talent for inventing mechanical

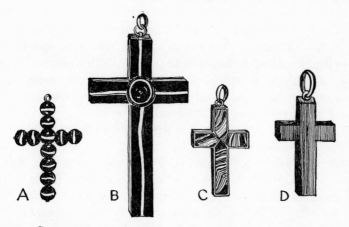

FIG. 24. Crosses, *c.*1870–80.
A. Onyx beads strung on wire. B. Onyx. C. Agate set in silver.
D. Bloodstone. *Collection of Mr & Mrs Penna*

techniques enabled them to copy supremely well. A good many crosses, such as one in pearls, gold and black enamel by John Brogden, were mourning jewellery and the shape of these later crosses (particularly the cheaper ones) suggests the tomb-stone rather than the Crucifix. The less expensive crosses of the 'seventies and 'eighties shew this most clearly. Figure 24 shews four of them, made in onyx and other semi-precious stones.

The fashion of necklace and matching cross, however, had

little to do with mourning—a fashion plate of the early 'eighties in the Victoria and Albert Museum shews three young women dressed for dinner, one of whom wears a loosely looped necklace of large round beads with a plain cross as pendant and two matching bracelets. The set is hand-coloured a rather crude red which suggests garnets. The rock crystal necklace and cross of Plate 28 shews a similar necklace, although this is the shorter collar shape which is slightly later. Mrs Flower shews a more opulent version—a photograph of a young lady in full evening dress *c.* 1887 in tiara, stomacher and shoulder knots as well as a collar necklace and large pendant cross, all in diamonds. The whole effect is remarkably secular and rather overwhelming.

In the last phase of Victoria's reign the Arts and Crafts jewellers produced some splendid crosses which were once again truly devotional in spirit. The cross had largely disappeared from fashionable commercial jewellery but these artist craftsmen made some very original *art nouveau* crosses. Henry Wilson's silver cross of *c.* 1890, its branches formed into the grape clusters of the True Vine, the cross itself hanging from a large baroque pearl, was particularly impressive. He also designed a shrine ring, with heavily jewelled bezel which was also a lid, opening to shew an enamelled panel of the Madonna and Child. The M for Mary brooches, for those with a special devotion to the Madonna, were a fashion of the early Romantic period of the 'forties and 'fifties. Pugin designed a beauty and the Castellani produced superb ones, closely following a medieval original (Plate 29).

Nonconformism during the Victorian period produced its own religious jewellery. Tiepins and brooches with a cameo portrait of John Wesley were worn as a sort of badge. A particularly fine agate portrait head mounted on a tiepin of *c.* 1850 is illustrated in Figure 25. Of their very nature, which tended to a puritan simplicity of manners, the great Evangelical movements of the century would not encourage anything more elaborate. The gravity which non-conformity induced was reflected in

ASBURY PARK PUBLIC LIBRARY

500 First Avenue
Asbury Park, NJ 07712-6193

Receipt

Date 4/3/98

_____

_____

FINES	
SALE BOOKS	50¢
MICROFILM	
SUBSCRIPTION CARDS	
LOST BORROWER'S CARDS	
LOST BOOKS	
PHOTOCOPIER	
OFFICE SUPPLIES	
INTERLIBRARY LOAN	
DONATIONS	
OTHER	

№ 6692   KB   TOTAL 50¢

F<small>IG</small>. 25. Tie Pin. Gold, with gem-stone cameo of John Wesley in blue-white agate, *c.*1850. *Collection of Mrs Bryan Pearce*

men's jewellery. A century which began with Beau Brummel and the dandies ended with subfusc attire and the cult of manly plainness. As Eastlake sadly observed in his *Household Taste*, 'Englishmen wear the same dress at an evening party as at a funeral.' 'We want,' he said, 'a style of dress which shall be at once picturesque and comfortable.' Men's jewellery followed the same progress. The early decades shew a certain spirit, but sobriety intervenes, to be followed by a reaction at the very end of the century, when a certain set in society practised a jaunty vulgarity.

The scope of male jewellery was whittled down during the century until it ended with cuff-links, tiepins, discreet signet or commemorative rings. At the beginning of Victoria's reign quizzing glasses on chains, breast pins, cravat pins which were almost as noticeable as female brooches, watch fobs and seals, tie and finger rings were worn. Jane Carlyle's description of Count D'Orsay's sartorial reaction to the approach of age describes fashions which were still anything but subfusc. 'In 1840 he had been as gay in his colours as a humming-bird—blue satin cravat, blue velvet waistcoat, cream coloured coat, trousers also of a bright colour . . . two glorious breast pins, attached by a chain, and length enough of gold-watch guard to hang himself in—today, in compliment to his five more years, he was all in black and brown—a black satin cravat, a brown velvet waistcoat, a brown coat . . . lined with velvet, and almost black trousers, one breast pin—a large pear-shaped pearl set into a little cup of diamonds—and only one fold of gold chain round his neck, tucked together right on the centre of his spacious breast with one magnificent turquoise.'

But in the early 'forties comparatively bright colours were still permissible for men. Two early portraits of Sir John Millais—in his Pre-Raphaelite days—one by Holman Hunt, shew him wearing soft silk cravat neck-ties, each secured by the same pin, a standing swan with its wings raised. The swan is quite large enough to be seen distinctly. Pins of the period 1840–50 are worth collecting. They can be slightly fantastic without being coy or vulgar. All the materials and techniques used in the female jewellery of the time were used—coral, pearl, garnet and pearl, cats' eyes, even mosaic and *pietra dura*. The jewellery of sentiment was represented by mourning tiepins edged in black enamels. Plates 15 and 20 and Figures 25 and 26 shew examples.

After this early period the tiepin almost but not quite

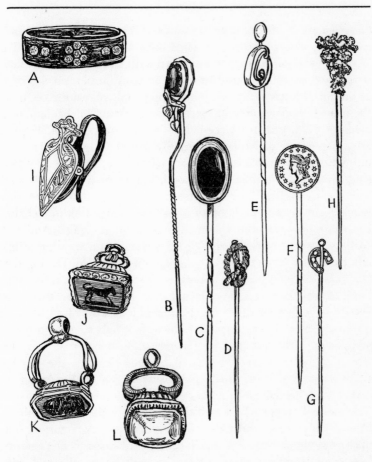

FIG. 26. Men's Jewellery:
A. Tie Ring, mock tortoise-shell with paste, *c.*1890. B. Cravat or Tie Pin, garnet and gold, *c.*1850. C. Onyx and gold, *c.*1870. D. Gold, in a sailor's knot, *c.*1896. E. Gold with pearl, *c.*1894. F. Gold with half dollar (date unreadable) c.1890. G. Pearl studded gold horseshoe, *c.*1890. H. With a gold nugget, *c.*1890. I. Buttonhole clip in silver, *c.*1890. J. and K. Two seals, *c.*1840. L. Gilt Fob with straw-coloured glass 'jewel', probably late Birmingham work. *Collections of Mr Louis Jolly and Miss Jenefer Peter*

disappeared. With the thin bow-ties of the 'sixties it was un-necessary, and the broad, starched turned-down collar (called a 'Shakespeare') also popular was worn with a broad tie controlled by a tie-ring. When these tie-rings turn up in old jewel-boxes or on the oddments tray of a junk-shop people may not recognize their function. They are oval, generally about an inch in diameter, made of gold, gilt, tortoise-shell or even mottled glass (Figure 26). A portrait of Millais in middle life at Wightwick shews him wearing a Shakespeare and very large tie, secured by a tie-ring decorated with a large diamond. Seal rings were sometimes used as tie-rings. There is also another type known as the Belcher Ring—a wide hoop of gold like a large link in a chain. By 1880 however the tiepin was in fashion again. Another Millais portrait of the early 'eighties shews him wearing a full silk tie with a large tiepin of onyx mounted in gold. During the last years of the century it appeared on sporting cravats—large, flash, diamond horse-shoes larger and more vulgar than the female jewellery of the time. Young bloods also often wore a gold coin as a tiepin, a spade guinea or a half sovereign were favourites. Amongst the increasing subfusc band of men to whom to be well-dressed was to be unnoticeable, the tiepin, when used at all, was small and discreet. But by the 'nineties men had collected quite a range of semi-precious accessories. The monocle replaced the quizzing glass, a walking cane might have a silver top, whilst the Birmingham jewellers turned out masses of cigarette cases, match cases, card cases, watch chains, buttonhole holders, cigar cutters, propelling pencils and cuff links, the larger surfaces of those in silver or gold plentifully engraved with weedy rococo curlicues.

Collar studs had appeared just before Victoria's reign began. Cuff links appeared at the end—in plain gold, often in onyx bordered with gold or even diamonds or garnets in very expensive sets. The bland expanse of the white evening shirt front was often decorated with a set of diamond, or in cheaper versions, paste buttons. These are worth acquiring to convert

into earrings. Women sometimes used cuff links on the very
severe blouses they wore with tailored suits in the 'nineties.
The cuff links illustrated, in silver with figures of the seasons,
were made for a female (Figure 28).

FIG. 27. Fob Jewel. Agate set in gold. An early and fine example,
*c.*1837. *Collection of Miss Josephine Harris*

FIG. 28. Cuff Links.
    A. Ladies', in silver representing the seasons, *c.*1899. B. Men's,
onyx and gold, *c.*1890. *Collection of Mrs Charles Girling*

The appearance and disappearance of the watch chain was a
fashion variation as changeable as the wearing of tiepins. As
late as 1845 seal fobs were worn hanging just below the short
waistcoat of the time, but fobs and chains were no longer
fashionable as items of display by the 'sixties (Figures 26, 27).
The longer coats covered them up. The watch chain displayed
from waistcoat pocket to button on mid-chest was a visible

feature in the later 'sixties, disappeared during the 'seventies and 'eighties and was fashionable again in the tight jacketed 'nineties. Whatever their date, these chains are nicely made and very useful worn as necklaces.

Through the period men wore rings, signet rings, seal rings, mourning rings and commemorative rings. These, slightly more plainly and heavily, followed the style of their period—the earliest having a trace of the eighteenth century still, whilst those of the 'nineties were so discreetly plain as to be uninteresting. Illustrated in Figure 8 is a heavy, gold finger ring with gipsy-set diamond, made of two wedding rings melted together. The MIZPAH ring in Figure 8 belonged to the same man. These two late Victorian men's rings in their plainness shew the sober jewellery permissible at the time. Signet rings in blood stone, onyx or cornelian had smaller less decorative bezels than before. The difference here between the comparative gaiety of the early years of the century and the last decades is most marked.

As gravity and sobriety was the ideal for the fathers (children, the Victorians said, should be seen and not heard), so Victorian children's jewellery was always on a simple and modest scale, avoided the vast excesses of adult fashion for that reason, and was often very pretty.

Little girls wore strings of beads, bracelets, lockets, brooches and chains, sometimes small light rings. A painting by Sir David Wilkie in the Tate, *The First Earring* (*c*. 1837) shews an apprehensive little girl of about eight having her ears pierced. Single gold hoops kept the holes open until the child wore her first proper earrings.

Infant jewellery started with corals which were given as a Christening present and these, because of their ancient protective function remained popular from beginning to end of the reign. Elaborate coral rattles mounted in silver (one with the figure of a little boy ringing a bell) were shewn at the Great Exhibition (Figure 29). Teething rings were also made of coral;

FIG. 29. Child's Coral. Set in silver. Exhibited at the Great Exhibition by Hilliard and Thomason, Birmingham

coral necklaces of branch coral or small coral beads, round or facetted and pairs of coral bracelets were worn by little children. A most delicate and pretty child's tiara in shell pink coral flowers and leaves (*c.* 1845) is to be seen in Birmingham Art Gallery (Plate 30). Later on the coral beads were larger and plainer, a little girl drawn by Millais in 1885, when she was about five, was wearing a short coral necklace of large round beads. Another Millais child (an illustration to *All Things Bright and Beautiful* in a children's song book) is shewn gathering rushes, wearing a long bead necklace and a heart-shaped locket. From the time of Tenniel's *Alice* illustrations children are shewn with these necklaces of large, plain beads. William Morris's family in a group photograph about 1870, has all three girls wearing bead necklaces, Jenny's the most grown up, longer, looped round several times and of much smaller, finer beads. Children also wore tiny crosses on a chain or ribbon. In the early period ribbon or velvet bracelets were worn, but from about 1860 the bracelets were more often of pearl, silver or beads. The romantic early period also saw little seed pearl necklaces for children and daisy-chains made of silver. Turquoise was another favourite material for children's jewellery (Figures 30, 31).

Fig. 30. Children's Jewellery Fashions:
A. 1840. B. 1854. C. *c.*1866–70. D. 1878. E. *c.*1890

By the 'nineties a new simplicity was gradually beginning to influence children's dress. Apart from simple brooches—flowers, Christian names, perhaps a plain silver bracelet—children were wearing very little jewellery. In *Seaton Court*, an improving children's story written at the end of the century, the heroine wore a flower with her party dress, no jewellery is mentioned. The sentimental romantic fantasy of the early period had utterly gone.

FIG. 31. Children's Jewellery:
  A. Ribbon Bracelet with miniature portrait set in gold, *c.*1840.
  B. One of a pair of coral Bracelets with gilt clasp, c.1850. c. Locket
  in turquoise *pavé* set in gold *c.*1860. D. Bracelet, silver, *c.*1890.
  Collections of Mr & Mrs Penna and Miss Jenefer Peter

The earlier romantic fantasies lingered longest in the very
cheapest jewellery: imported mock jet which was black and
shiny glass and flashing glass beads from Bohemia and Ger-
many. Cut steel, which was used for buckles, could make
flashing parures (Plate 31). The Birmingham toymakers were
a repository of old patterns, no longer high fashion. As late as
1906, the pattern book of a manufacturer of electro-type gilt
buckles and clasps in Birmingham shews clasps like Neo-
Etruscan *bulla* brooches to be stamped out by the hundred.
Some of these designs have a folk-art straightforwardness which
is charming. They may be seen in Birmingham Art Gallery. A
pair of earrings, probably bought at a fair-ground, very glittery
in ruby and colourless cut glass perhaps 1850, perhaps much
later, are shewn in Plate 32. They have an artless charm, like
that of the bright rustic ornaments which decorated cottage
kitchens at the time.

Index

97

Index